YOU WERE BORN FOR A REASON
The Real Purpose of Life

YOU WERE BORN FOR A REASON

The Real Purpose of Life

Kentetsu Takamori
Daiji Akehashi
Kentaro Ito

Translated and adapted by
Juliet Winters Carpenter

Translation supervised by
Edward G. Seidensticker

Ichimannendo Publishing, Inc.
Los Angeles   Tokyo

You Were Born for a Reason: The Real Purpose of Life
By Kentetsu Takamori, Daiji Akehashi, and Kentaro Ito
Published by Ichimannendo Publishing, Inc. (IPI)
19750 S. Vermont Ave., Suite 200, Torrance, California 90502
info@i-ipi.com   www.i-ipi.com
© 2006 by Kentetsu Takamori, Daiji Akehashi, and Kentaro Ito. All rights reserved.
Translated and adapted by Juliet Winters Carpenter, under the supervision of Edward G. Seidensticker.
All translations throughout this book, unless otherwise noted, are by Juliet Winters Carpenter.

NOTE TO THE READER:
In the process of producing the English translation, this book was widely adapted by the authors in close collaboration with the translator.
Throughout this work, Japanese names are given in Western order. However, names of historical and literary figures who lived prior to the Meiji era (before 1868) are given in traditional Japanese order, family name first.

Jacket design by Kazumi Endo
Photographs by Sebun Photo (Kaoru Sunatsubo, jacket; Asoo Fujita, p. 1; Mitsushi Okada, p. 45)

First edition, November 2006
Printed in Japan
11 10 09 08   3 4 5 6 7 8 9 10

No part of this book may be reproduced in any form without permission from the publisher.

This book was originally published in Japanese by Ichimannendo Publishing under the title *Naze Ikiru.*
© 2001 by Kentetsu Takamori, Daiji Akehashi, and Kentaro Ito

"About Schmidt"
Copyright MMII, New Line Productions, Inc.
All rights reserved. Dialogue appears courtesy of New Line Productions, Inc.

"Can't Help Falling In Love"
Words and music by George David Weiss, Hugo Peretti and Luigi Creatore.
Copyright © 1961 by Gladys Music, Inc. Copyright renewed and assigned to Gladys Music.
All rights administered by Cherry Lane Music Publishing Company, Inc. and Chrysalis Music.
International copyright secured. All rights reserved.

"Yesterday"
Copyright © 1965 Sony/ATV Tunes LLC. All rights administered by Sony/ATV Music Publishing, 8 Music Square West, Nashville, TN 37203. All rights reserved. Used by permission.
© 1965 Sony/ATV Tunes LLC (Renewed). All rights administered by Sony/ATV Music Publishing, 8 Music Square West, Nashville, TN 37203. All rights reserved. Used by permission.
The rights for Japan licensed to Sony Music Publishing (Japan) Inc.
JASRAC 出 0615268-601

Distributed in the United States and Canada by Ichimannendo Publishing, Inc. (IPI)
19750 S. Vermont Ave., Suite 200, Torrance, California 90502
Distributed in Japan by Ichimannendo Publishing
2-4-5F Kanda-Ogawamachi, Chiyoda-ku, Tokyo 101-0052
info@10000nen.com   www.10000nen.com

Library of Congress Control Number: 2006936135
ISBN-13 978-0-9790471-0-7
ISBN-10 0-9790471-0-2

ISBN 4-925253-24-7

Contents

Part Two
The Words of Shinran

Introduction

Today in countries around the world, people enjoy wealth and comfort unheard of in centuries past. Medical and scientific advances mean that we live longer and have greater ability to change and control our environment to suit our needs. But have these advances brought greater happiness? Modern society is plagued with ills such as violence in its many forms, including tyranny, terrorism, murder, and suicide. Real answers to these problems continue to elude us.

Our advances may have made us richer, but they have not done anything to ensure our happiness or provide us with a sense of abiding meaningfulness. In fact, modern life often seems only to bring more acute feelings of isolation, loneliness, and emptiness.

Why is it that, although blessed with physical health and an abundant lifestyle, we cannot find heart's ease?

This question was addressed more than twenty-five hundred years ago in India by Siddhārtha Gautama (Śākyamuni), the founder of Buddhism. Born a prince, he excelled from boyhood in literary and military arts; he wedded the loveliest young woman in the kingdom; he lacked for nothing. Yet his heart was not cheered in the least. He passed the days despondently, knowing that even though good health, treasure, status, honor, family, and talent were his, he would one day lose them all: no earthly happiness could prevail over old age, sickness, and death. Realizing the nature of human existence, Siddhārtha was unable to experience true ease or satisfaction.

Finally, when he was twenty-nine years old, he crept out of the palace one night in search of true happiness. For six years he lived the life of a mountain ascetic, until his eyes were opened to the truth that all people can obtain absolute happiness, and he achieved Buddhahood.

The lessons taught by Śākyamuni Buddha are timelessly true. We all are vulnerable to the devastation of sudden illness striking oneself or a loved one. And although we may immerse ourselves in work or a hobby, the day will come when old age prevents us from enjoying such activities. When we die, moreover, we must part from those we love. What is there in life that will never betray us, that we can devote ourselves to without regret? Throughout his life, Śākyamuni continued to teach that the purpose of life is none other than to gain unassailable, eternal happiness. In Japan, the essence of this message was preached by Shinran (1173–1263), the founder of Shin Buddhism (the True Pure Land School).

Shinran laid out the purpose of life and urged its attainment with incomparable clarity: The universal purpose of life is to destroy the root of suffering and gain joy in being alive, so that you rejoice at having been born human and live on in eternal happiness. No matter how hard your life may be, keep on until you accomplish this purpose. The nine decades of his life were focused single-mindedly on this message.

Yet mankind today remains lost in the dark, ignorant of life's purpose and unsure whether life has any meaning.

War, murder, suicide, violence, abuse—could it be that all such tragedies arise out of the darkness of mind that cannot make sense of life, or find any reason to go on living? Simply lowering the legal age of criminal responsibility is not a solution, since it will not reform the hearts of these young offenders who have no awareness of their wrongdoing. These terrible blights on society will resist all countermeasures unless the dignity and purpose of life are made clear. Until that happens, any action is as futile and transitory as drawing pictures on the water.

Is there a purpose in life, or not?

What is the meaning of life?

These age-old questions cry out for clear answers. Shinran stated the purpose of life more plainly than ever before, and urged its attainment. He is indeed the light of the world that breaks through the dark delusions of the human race.

Is there a purpose in life? In this book we will address this question head-on, through the prism of Shinran's words. We begin in Part One by examining the human condition, along with the comments of leading writers, thinkers, and newsmakers from East and West. In Part Two we turn to quotations from Shinran's teachings that demonstrate the unchanging, timeless purpose of life, with paraphrase and commentary as aids in understanding.

Across the centuries, the words of Shinran have helped untold millions in Japan to hear the message of life's purpose. It is our great hope and dream that this book may convey his words to millions more around the world, so that they too may enter into true and lasting happiness.

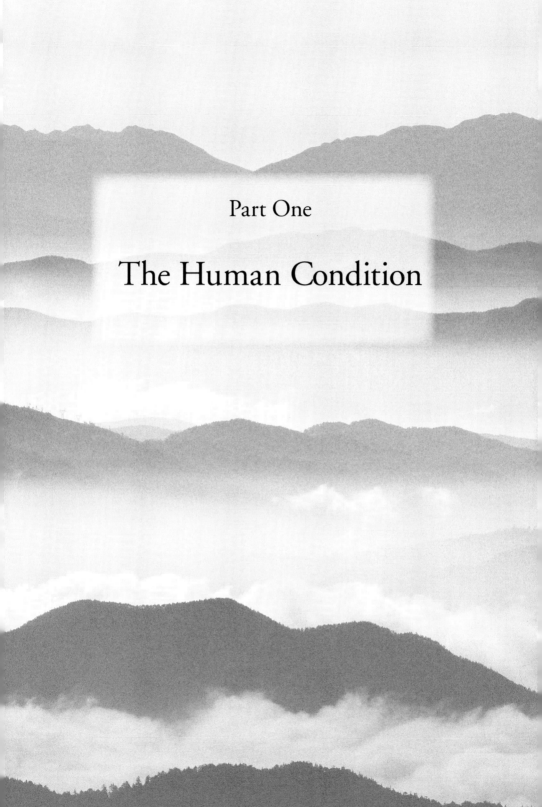

Part One

The Human Condition

CHAPTER 1

The Fragility of Happiness

"Get out!"

Mother ran downstairs and hammered Father with her fists, shrieking at him to leave. The sound rings in my ears to this day. As I stood rooted to the spot, Father passed wordlessly in front of me and on out the door, never to return. I was in grade school. It was months before I learned the word "divorce" and understood the sad situation. Through tears, I grasped the hard truth that happiness can collapse and disappear in an instant, without the slightest warning.

As that boy learned to his sorrow, even the most apparently secure happiness may crumble at any time.[1] Life is uncertain, apt to spring a nasty surprise when we least expect it. What's the point of it all? What is life all about, anyway? When we find ourselves shaken out of the lull of routine, standing aghast like the little boy above, questions like these demand serious answers.

Bookstores and libraries overflow with stories of people who have overcome all manner of adversity and found happiness through their tenacity and their strength of will. These books encourage us to keep going: "Happiness can be yours!" "Find your passion and follow it, whatever it might be." All of these success stories tell us to keep moving forward, step by step. But what direction are we to take, and where are we headed? Those answers are not necessarily clear.

EVERY ACTION HAS ITS PURPOSE

Every action has a definite purpose. Riding in a taxi, for instance, even the quietest person speaks up without hesitation to tell the driver his destination. Otherwise, the driver would have no idea which way to go. Heading off in a direction chosen at random would be a waste of time and money.

Ask someone why he is studying, and he is likely to mention a test the next day, or talk about getting his license. Ask someone where she is off to, and she may say she is going shopping, or out for a breath of fresh air. All our actions have a purpose.

What if someone asked you the point of living? What would you answer?

Certainly, life is far from easy. The modern workplace, for instance, brings its own difficulties and stresses. In her book *White-Collar Sweat-shop*, Jill Andresky Fraser writes of new difficulties that have faced American workers during the last two decades, in which layoffs have become commonplace despite ongoing economic prosperity. She points out that young workers of today have little job security or guarantee of career advancement; that in midlife they are torn by the conflicting demands of work, children, and aging parents; and that in later life, despite expectations that they will be rewarded for all their years of hard work, men and women are often let go, with bleak prospects for their remaining years.[2]

Why must we endure these hardships to go on living? Others may advise us to "hang in there," "fight the good fight," and "never say die," but if they cannot offer us any clear and compelling reason to live, these words fall flat. However well-intentioned, such platitudes can feel like the crack of a whip as we run in endless circles.

WHEN LIFE BECOMES PREDICTABLE

In Aesop's fable of the ant and the grasshopper, the ant toiled all summer and then was able to kick up its heels and enjoy life in the winter. Most of us do not enjoy that luxury. Instead, we slave away in all seasons, year in and year out. On the way to work, day after day we may pass the same people in the same places, until their faces become vaguely familiar. They, like us, are committed to an unvarying routine.

Without lasting joy or fulfillment in living, the days merge into one indistinguishable blur of eating, sleeping, and getting up. Living such a life is like running a footrace with no goal: without the thrill of anticipation or the joy of crossing the finish line, why strain to keep up the pace? In life, too, only those with a clear sense of direction and purpose can stay the course with vigor.

KNOWING LIFE'S PURPOSE MAKES ALL THE DIFFERENCE

Knowing life's purpose would invest everything one did with meaning. Whether reading a book, performing a task, or caring for one's health, one would feel deep commitment and satisfaction. Even if one were suffering from a dreadful disease, enmeshed in a family quarrel, or stung by a humiliating defeat, the power to live—the determination to overcome any obstacle in order to fulfill life's great purpose—would always come flooding back. In his *On the Genealogy of Morals*, Friedrich Nietzsche (1844–1900) effectively underscored the importance of meaning in life when he wrote that man desires suffering and "even seeks it out, provided that he has been shown a *meaning* for it, a *reason* for suffering."[3]

The road stretching ahead may be long, but face the right direction and any forward motion will bring one that much closer to the goal, with no waste of energy. Whatever it costs in time or strength or money to realize the purpose of life will certainly be rewarded in full. No experience is ever thrown away or lost. Even those engulfed in wave after wave of sorrow are sure to find their reward, once they know the ultimate purpose of living.

Some declare life to be wonderful and fulfilling, while others decry it as empty and meaningless. What makes the difference? Simply knowing life's true purpose.

THE "HEAVINESS" OF HUMAN LIFE

In cases of shipwrecks or other disasters, entire rescue squads are often mobilized to save a single life. That is because each life has inestimable value; in the words of the German poet Rainer Maria Rilke (1875–1926), "Life is heavier than the heaviness of all things."[4] If the innate goodness of life were not a given, then the practice of medicine would collapse, along with politics, economics, science, the arts, ethics, and law—all of which are nothing more or less than different approaches to the goal of living a longer and happier life.

Each field has its own way of enhancing the quality of life. It is the role of politics and economics to explore ways for people to live at ease, unconcerned by threats of layoffs or expensive nursing care. Breakthroughs in science and technology, meanwhile, have made life easier than ever before: Doing the laundry used to be backbreaking labor that entailed bending over a washtub, scrubbing wet clothes on a washboard, and wringing them tightly, but today all it takes is the push of a button. Finding ways to resolve interpersonal conflict and allow neighbors to live peaceably together is the sphere of ethics and law. And because the prospect of work, work, work without relief is unbearable, sports and the arts exist to invigorate us. Each of these fields of endeavor is concerned with how to surmount the hardships of life and find pleasure in living. Even altruistic contributions to the greater happiness of humanity comprise a *way of living* rather than an ultimate *purpose of life*.

THE STRUGGLE TO OVERCOME ILLNESS

In the front lines of medicine, hard-fought battles are taking place to extend human life. For organ transplants from brain-dead patients, teams of physicians work together with split-second timing, removing the organs and packing them in ice so they can be airlifted by helicopter or plane. The heart must be transplanted within four hours, so there is literally not a second to spare. The total cost of a transplant, from determination of brain death through postsurgical monitoring, runs to hundreds of thousands of dollars.

But if that same life is doomed to disappear without trace in the end, why go to such extreme measures to preserve it? One heart transplant patient, asked by a newspaper reporter what he planned to do with his new lease on life, answered, "Drink beer and go to night baseball games." Another man living overseas, desperately sick, raised the necessary funds through the goodwill donations of strangers and traveled to the United States to await a donor—only to cause widespread outrage after his successful transplant by refusing to return to work and instead choosing to spend his days gambling. It is hard not to sympathize with one indignant supporter who snorted that he felt foolish for having donated so much money.

We are glad to see scientific advances that extend the average human lifespan. But the question then arises, "What will people do with the extra time they have been given?" Ethical debate over organ transplants revolves around secondary issues like confirming the will of the donor, ensuring fairness in access to the pool of organs, or setting and enforcing standards for determination of brain death, while the fundamental question—"Why resort to such extraordinary measures in order to keep people alive?"—goes unasked.

The goal of suffering in order to combat disease must be not merely life, but happiness. Treatment that serves simply to prolong suffering is meaningless. But what if people used their extra time on earth to fulfill the purpose of life and know the joy of living? Would not today's lifesaving medical practices then be truly wonderful?

We are continually surrounded by a chorus of voices urging us to live and persevere, yet no one stops to consider or thinks to ask why, if life is so painful, we are bound to go on living. Could anything be more mysterious?

CHAPTER 2

The Infinite Preciousness of a Single Human Life

"It's great to be alive!" How many people live this way, overflowing with good spirits and optimism? The twentieth century, when technology advanced rapidly but true abundance lagged behind, has been characterized as an age of anxiety. Blessed with material goods, many people lack for nothing, yet deep down they are discontent, filled with a vague, pervasive sense of unease and emptiness.

> Life is vaguely pleasant in its way, and fulfilling. But in its way it is also a bore. Day after day, the same routine … On the way home after a hard day's work, jostled in a crowded commuter train, the tired businessperson or secretary lets out a sigh. Or the harried housewife, caught between the demands of housework and childcare, stops for a brief rest. It is at such moments, amid the seeming contentment of busy days, that a sudden void opens in the heart. And then the silent murmur starts up: "My life was never meant to be this way. What if it goes on like this to the bitter end? What's the point?"[5]

Viktor Frankl—one of the greatest minds of the twentieth century; the Austrian neurologist, psychiatrist, and philosopher—pointed out that modern man, the moment he is freed from busyness to do at last whatever he wants, often feels that his life is meaningless and empty. People who retire lose their bearings; college students get drunk on weekends; night after night, we sit passively before the television set.

Frankl went on to say that the reason many people today are beset with a sense of emptiness is that they do not know why they are alive. This state he called an "existential vacuum." Often this existential vacuum leads to suicide. Other widespread ills such as depression, aggression, and addiction can only be understood when we recognize the existential vacuum beneath them. The same can be said for crises of retirement and aging.[6]

Many people have noted that those unable to find meaning or value in their lives are on the increase, a factor behind various problems in society. Even the young are affected. According to the National Institute of Mental Health, suicide was the third leading cause of death among people aged ten through twenty-four in the U.S. in 2000.[7] Each year in the U.S., approximately two million adolescents attempt suicide, and approximately two thousand youths aged ten through nineteen succeed in killing themselves.[8]

WHY IS IT WRONG TO KILL?

Often young people show as little regard for the lives of others as for their own. In 1997 in Connecticut, ex-Marine Todd Rizzo, who was then eighteen, bludgeoned Stanley Edwards IV, who was thirteen, to death with a sledgehammer. He later told the authorities he needed to know what it would be like to kill.

In London in 2004, a gang of four young people, including a teenage girl, was arrested for attacking a thirty-seven-year-old man seated on a bench; they killed him by kicking his head "like a football." They sought not money but rather entertainment, taking pleasure in inflicting pain and humiliation on random strangers; as the gang leader admitted after his arrest for murder, "It could have been anybody." Using the latest video mobile phones, the gang recorded these acts of feral cruelty—including the horrified reactions of hapless victims—so they could replay them later or send them to friends. This phenomenon, known as "happy slapping," seems to have originated in South London, but it has now spread to the rest of England and to other countries in Europe as well.

Similarly, "bum hunting," attacks on the homeless committed by teenagers and young adults, is on the rise in the U.S., as in Japan and the U.K. Advocates for the homeless say that such terrorizing is motivated by a combination of thrill-seeking and contempt for the down-and-out. According to Michael Stoops, executive director of the National Coalition for the Homeless, "They do this because they think they can, that they can get away with beating a homeless person and nobody will care, and the homeless won't be able to fight back."[9] The coalition has documented 386 attacks on the homeless over the past six years, including 156 deaths. Of the total number of attacks, 211 have been recorded since 2002.

Sometimes, of course, the attacker chooses someone he knows. In 1997, in a horrific incident that was unprecedented in Japan, a fourteen-year-old boy in Kobe killed and decapitated an eleven-year-old friend and left the head at the gate of his, the killer's, school. Yet a few days after the murder, when the killer sent a letter to the local newspaper in which he referred to himself as an "invisible person," this phrase struck a chord with many teenagers.

Youngsters like these may feel as useless as yesterday's trash, and wish they had never been born. Life becomes a burden, something to get over with as quickly as possible.

Absent a sense of the preciousness of one's own life, why respect the life of anyone else? The voice that whispers "Why not die?" is not far from asking, "Why not kill?" Indeed, one in four youths who commit suicide injure or kill someone else before their suicide.[10]

Nevertheless, most people would agree with Rilke that "life is heavier than the heaviness of all things." We feel strongly that every human life is uniquely precious, without being able to explain just why. Philosophers are no less stumped. Philippa Foot, professor emeritus of philosophy at the University of California, Los Angeles, wrote in "Moral Relativism" that she knows of no philosopher who has ever been able to explain the value of human life.[11] Reading hundreds of philosophy tomes would bring us no closer to an answer.

INCREASING SUICIDE RATES

It is not only young people who take their own lives. For years, Japanese have enjoyed the longest lifespans on the planet—and yet, more than thirty thousand Japanese kill themselves every year, making Japan's the highest suicide rate per capita in the developed world. The number of suicides in Japan is more than four times the number of traffic accident victims per year. In 1998, a sudden jump in male suicides actually lowered the average life expectancy for Japanese men.

Some have suggested that the rising incidence of suicide in Japan is linked to the lingering economic difficulties plaguing the nation since the late 1980s, but this explanation is far too simplistic. French sociologist Emile Durkheim (1858–1917) showed the incidence of suicide to be highest among people of independent means, and provided a wide array of statistics to back his assertion that "the possessors of most comfort suffer most."[12]

Mere access to entertainment and labor-saving devices cannot assuage people's deepest needs. It is not ease that we crave, but meaning and purpose. The renowned American psychologist Mihaly Csikszentmihalyi has stated that without a profound purpose in life, people cannot obtain true satisfaction, no matter what conveniences and entertainment may surround them.[13]

The underlying cause of suicide is failure to understand the importance of life's purpose and the dignity of human life. Overwhelmed with pain and despair, the sufferer asks, "Why go on living at such a cost? What's the use?" Under these conditions, it is no surprise if ignorance concerning the fundamental purpose of life should lead many to choose self-inflicted oblivion.

The winning ticket to a multimillion-dollar lottery is prized because its owner knows that it represents more than a lifetime's earnings; a losing ticket goes straight into the wastebasket. Things of no value, whether chipped cups or computers damaged beyond repair, are unceremoniously dumped. No one who understood the infinite preciousness of his life would ever jump off a tall building—throwing that life away like a losing lottery ticket—or callously stamp out the life of another.

The high rate of suicide among young people, along with the escalating rate of murders in that age group, has thrown modern society into turmoil. Many factors can be cited in this increasing violence: the breakdown of the family, the failure of the school system, antiquated laws, society itself. But until we focus on the essential purpose of life, all such debate is empty and can offer no remedy. Human life has a definite purpose that must be accomplished. To that end, we each must live out our life to the full, however painful that may be. When we gain a clear understanding of the purpose of life, the dignity of life is revealed.

THE HEART PARCHED FOR MEANING

The most serious terrorist attack in Japan's modern history occurred in March 1995, causing massive disruption and widespread fear. Five members of the Aum Supreme Truth cult released the deadly nerve agent sarin in five subway trains in Tokyo, resulting in twelve dead and more than five thousand injured. One youth later explained why he had joined the cult: "Only [cult founder Shoko] Asahara dealt straight on with the meaning of my existence." Parched for clarity, he settled for muddy water.

The five perpetrators included bright young graduates of Japan's most elite universities—including the alma mater of one of the authors of this book, who was a student at the time.[14] After the incident, he attended classes expecting to hear professors seriously address, and perhaps even assume a measure of responsibility for, the horrendous act of mass murder carried out by one of the university's own. In every case, however, classes proceeded as usual. Only one professor made an exceedingly indirect and offhand reference to the incident, wondering aloud what could ever have attracted anyone to a religious founder so "dirty-looking." This irresponsible demonstration of unconcern by intellectuals uniquely positioned to speak out with authority was a great disappointment. But it also goes a long way toward explaining why it is that despite all our modern scientific advances, divination and fortune-telling remain popular, and superstition and false religions continue to flourish: they provide a semblance of guidance and meaning, something to fill the void.

When will people understand the true value of human life?

CHAPTER 3

Living Simply for the Sake of Living

SOLDIERING ON

Some might argue that the purpose of life is simply to live—that living is, in itself, meaning enough. Let us examine this assertion. If we interpret it as, "just bear up and get on with your life," then many people might agree. Their advice would be, "Whatever happens, keep a stiff upper lip and soldier on. You only live once, so make the most of it. Life itself is infinitely valuable." Even someone unsure of the meaning of life might find a measure of comfort in the notion that just being alive is in itself reason enough to live.

But for anyone who is truly suffering and who questions why life must go on, news that the purpose of life is "to live" would have to come as a disappointment. That is because it is no answer at all.

Think about it for a moment. If you asked a jogger, "Why do you jog?" and he said "To build up my strength," the answer would make perfect sense, but if he said "I jog for the sake of jogging," you would be left scratching your head. Or if you asked high school students what motivates them to study for the SATs and they said "We want to get into college," you would fully accept that answer, while "We study for the SATs for the sake of studying for the SATs" would be sheer nonsense. In the same way, the question "Why do you live?" cannot be answered "I live for the sake of living," because that is a meaningless tautology.

THE NEED FOR A PURPOSE IN LIFE

Life progresses steadily from yesterday to today and from today to to-morrow. "Time flies like an arrow," goes the saying, and perhaps it is true that we rush along at breakneck speed. We move from one generally accepted goal to the next throughout our lives. As children, we progress from one grade level to the next, up through elementary, middle, and high school; many go on to college almost automatically; and when we move into the workforce, problems at work consume all our energy. From the moment we are thrown into life's rough waters, we are forced to keep on swimming. Finally, in midlife, we take stock and wonder, "Is this all there is? Is this what I have been working for all this time?"

Since living is in a sense like swimming, the person who declares, "I live for the sake of living," is no different than one who declares, "I swim for the sake of swimming." But what happens to a weed floating on the surface of the ocean? It is carried aimlessly back and forth on the waves until it begins to decay. The misfortune of a swimmer with no purpose or goal is clear.

Or the life of such a person could be likened to the flight path of an airplane that is "flying for the sake of flying." Think about it. Decisions about speed and altitude, route alterations based on changes in wind or air pressure, responses to engine trouble—all these are choices that affect the "how-to" of flight. What must be known before any of these decisions are made is the destination, since this will determine the direction, or the "where-to," of flight. What pilot in his right mind would take off without having a destination? An airplane flying only for the sake of flying is doomed to crash. In the same way, without a purpose that imparts lasting satisfaction and joy, would we not find, at death, that life had been nothing but an endless chain of suffering?

CHAPTER 4

Temporary Pleasures

PLEASURE GROWN OLD IS PAIN

Today, people with the determination to know and to carry out their larger task in life are a vanishing breed. Scientific civilization has destroyed more than the natural environment, it would seem, as more and more people seek salvation in pleasures of the moment. Too often, they are overwhelmed by them. One sign of this is the prevalence of the word "compulsive," along with the suffix "-holic," both of which have acquired great currency. They are used to refer to people with uncontrollable drives or fixations, people who cannot rest unless engaged in a particular activity.

Today, millions of Americans have fallen prey to one such debilitating disorder or another.

> For example, reportedly 10 percent of Americans, or 20 million, suffer from alcoholism. And this 20 million is small compared with the 80 million made codependent by their familial association. The number of gamblers is estimated at 20 million, matching the number of alcoholics. Compulsive eaters number some 30 million, 80 million if the obese are included. Sex addiction apparently plagues 25 million Americans. The compulsive-shopping population is estimated at 15 million, or 40 million when those afflicted with overspending

are included … The discovery of new addictions, disorders, and compulsions and their seeming ubiquity has become a staple of our daily news.[15]

Drug sales and gang activity have now begun to invade even the elementary schools, and use of narcotics causes addicts to commit increasingly horrific crimes. Still other people cannot bear to be alone, and rush into physical relationships with many and unspecified partners; for them, sexual intimacy is a means of staving off a deep emptiness. Such syndromes are an expression of pain so great that sufferers require diversion simply to go on living. They provide not ultimate meaning, but temporary escape.

Someone may protest, "So what? People should do whatever gives them the most pleasure at any given time. The pleasure of the moment is reason enough for being. The hell with trying to figure out what grand purpose it all adds up to. Better forget about the whole thing and just have fun."

Yet is it really possible to live for pleasure? Let us take a look at the true nature of pleasure. First, there is the pleasure of satisfying a desire. Human desires come in an endless variety of forms: the desire to eat well or dress fashionably, the yearning for a car or a lover. As a desire is satisfied, discontent and pain go away, and the agreeable sensation experienced in the process is what we find gratifying.

For example, when you are thirsty and take a drink of Coca-Cola, you immediately experience the "pause that refreshes." That initial burst of pleasure is ephemeral, however. As one sip follows another, your thirst is gradually relieved, and the sense of exhilaration declines proportionally. What you are actually enjoying is the process of your thirst lessening. In the total absence of thirst, drinking a Coca-Cola (or any other drink) would turn into a rather painful experience. It is exactly like scratching an itch—keep it up too long, and the place will stop feeling good and start to hurt instead.

Where dissatisfaction ends, pain begins. This well-known phenomenon, known to economists as the law of diminishing marginal utility, is observable in all sorts of situations. The thrill of a date, or of a new hobby, wears off inevitably with repetition. The agreeable sensation obtained from gratification of a desire can reach intense euphoria, but it is doomed to vanish in the end. That is why it is said that the early stage of pain is pleasure, and pleasure grown old is pain.

MOMENTS OF ESCAPE

Many people would say they are happiest when engrossed in a hobby. Challenging a swimming record, reading an opponent's chess moves, finding secure foot-rests while rock climbing: at times like these, whether the goal is victory or survival, the mind focuses intently on the task at hand, undistracted by pent-up feelings on irrelevant matters such as the terrible thing someone said recently, the boss's outburst, or an upcoming meeting with someone you dislike. You are "in the zone," carried along in the flow of things, thinking of nothing else.

But since the pleasure of a hobby or other fulfilling activity is temporary, like the satisfaction obtained from gratifying a desire, once it is over you are confronted once again with grim reality in the form of tiresome homework, an overflowing inbox, or piled-up household chores. That may explain why a certain famous tennis player was known for his foul temper off the tennis court, and why Pablo Picasso was said to be out of humor the moment he laid down his brush, however happily he had been painting.

In *The Conquest of Happiness*, philosopher Bertrand Russell wrote, "Fads and hobbies … are in many cases, perhaps most, not a source of fundamental happiness, but a means of escape from reality, of forgetting for the moment some pain too difficult to be faced."[16] The pleasure of losing oneself in a hobby is thus a way of killing time to gain a temporary diversion from pain. It is much like the drunkard who is able to forget his debts and enjoy himself only when he is in his cups.

Someone may scoff, "So what? Trying to figure out the meaning of life is depressing. Why not immerse myself in something I enjoy, have some fun? That's enough for me." Yet—to continue the analogy between hobbies and alcohol—that is like saying, "Nothing tastes as good as alcohol. Life is nothing without it. Anyone who doesn't drink is a fool."

In fact, there are people who declare, "Who needs alcohol or drugs when life itself is wonderful!" Once you have found the purpose of life, then you no longer need to hide your pain and loneliness. Indeed, when you attain the purpose of life, each passing moment becomes more radiant than all the stars in the sky.

SOME SAY THE DESTINATION IS NOT IMPORTANT

A scholar absorbed in research or an athlete focused on her game takes pleasure in research or movement for its own sake. Whether his conclusions are recognized or not, whether her team wins the tournament or not, is secondary at best. In the pursuit of truth or the attempt to shatter a record, it is the *process of seeking* that brings joy and meaning to life: for many people, this is a basic, fundamental belief.

We admire people with the energy and commitment to single-mindedly devote their lives to something that they love. This is especially true in this age of postmodern disillusionment, when many people feel that their lives lead nowhere, and that they cannot break out of this cycle of helplessness.

Even if you do embark on an endeavor that you feel invests your life with meaning, can you be certain it will last? In 1992, at the Barcelona Olympic Games, fourteen-year-old swimmer Kyoko Iwasaki skyrocketed to world fame by capturing the gold medal in the breaststroke event. She expressed her rapture in these words: "This is the happiest thing in my whole life!" At just fourteen, she had experienced one of the greatest joys that life could offer. Naturally, expectations were high for her to repeat the feat at the next Olympic Games. The pressure was enormous, but she was so busy with her studies that she was unable to practice, and went into a slump. In talking about how she felt as she contemplated giving up swimming, she made this confession: "While I was worrying about whether I'd be able to go to the Games in Atlanta or not, I used to think, 'Oh, I should never have said Barcelona was the happiest thing in my life.' I didn't even want the gold medal anymore."[17]

What had been the "happiest thing" for Iwasaki became something she "didn't even want." She barely managed to qualify for the Atlanta Games, and placed tenth. After that she lost all interest in competition, and dropped out with no apparent regrets.

In the academic world, of all who devote themselves to research, barely a handful carve out a name in history. Yet Charles Darwin, who devoted his life to developing the theory of evolution, gained no happiness from his historic achievement. He lamented having become "a kind of machine for grinding general laws out of large collections of facts."[18]

Even the pleasure of pursuing one's chosen path goes stale in the end.

"I enjoy following the path I am on; it doesn't matter where it leads." Some people might be satisfied with this outlook. But what is missing from this view? As Durkheim points out in his work *Suicide*, without an attainable goal, the act of walking is pleasurable only so long as we remain blind to its uselessness.[19]

Tomorrow, and the next day, and the next, tumble one after another down time's long stairs—and, in the words of the seventeenth-century French philosopher Blaise Pascal, "The last act is tragic, however happy all the rest of the play is."[20] The most beautiful life is no exception. Its ending—death—is a foregone conclusion.

After casting a dispassionate eye on where we have come from and where we are headed, how could anyone claim that a life of endless seeking, or the simple act of walking without a goal, could bring lasting pleasure?

CHAPTER 5

Work, Work, Work

It is often said that a fulfilling job is the purpose of life. Yet how many of us actually find our work fulfilling? Even successful people who are able to showcase their talents run up against hard realities that prevent them from doing as they wish. Some celebrities, for instance, feel so acutely the pain of the loss of their privacy that it can begin to sour even the extraordinary career that brought them fame in the first place.

Basketball great Michael Jordan is one of the most appealing and charismatic figures in the sports world. But his enormous celebrity has come with a price; he is a virtual prisoner of his fame. Going out in public causes such a stir among his fans that, when possible, he says he prefers to stay home or in a hotel room.

His perfect day, he says, would be to get up and take his wife and children to a pancake house for breakfast and then go to an amusement park, something he says he hasn't done since he was twelve or thirteen years old.

"I can't go," he says in his book *Rare Air*, published in 1993, at about the height of his fame. "I can, but I don't want to go through the [whole] spectacle. It's not fair to the children … Sometimes I wonder what it would be like not to be Michael Jordan. Or to be Michael Jordan, but to be just like everyone else who has a family and is able to do family things."[21]

An extraordinary man, he seeks an ordinary life.

Meanwhile, fiction writer Haruki Murakami—whose work has been translated into about forty languages—is adamant that he has not gained any release or relief through writing books:

> I do not write and publish sketches like this to make myself feel better … At least so far, I see no sign that writing has been at all liberating to my spirit … People write because they can't help themselves. The act of writing is of no use in itself, and provides no attendant salvation.[22]

Guy de Maupassant, the French master of the short story, said: "Do not envy the writer, but rather pity him."

However much you may love and excel at something, when you make it your job, it can quickly turn into a burden. Even people whose work attracts admiration and envy must carry an unseen load of sorrow and distress.

SELLING OFF OUR LIVES

Though written over fifty years ago, the Pulitzer Prize–winning play *Death of a Salesman* by Arthur Miller continues to be performed—often by some of the best stage actors of our day—and remains relevant. The main character, Willy Loman, is a traveling salesman beset with mortgage payments, household repairs, and worn-out home appliances. Unable to withstand the toll of passing years, he is forced to watch his salary dwindle as his sales record plummets. One day he muses to his wife, "Figure it out. Work a lifetime to pay off a house. You finally own it, and there's nobody to live in it."[23] Eventually he is fired and, unable to cope with crushing burdens, takes his own life. The insurance will cover Willy's debts, but Willy himself is no longer around. The play does not make clear what commodity it was that he sold; that is because he sold his very life.

Each person's life is the time allotted him or her. For lucky infants in Japan, where longevity is at record levels, this can mean a gift of eighty years or more. What should such a treasure be spent on? The college student who takes a part-time job to pay for a trip abroad wears away his or her life by just that much. Bit by bit, we sell off our lives to obtain the things we want.

Willy Loman works himself to a state of exhaustion, but is fired anyway. Forsaken by his employer and his two sons, he dies a lonely death. Not even his wife can save him. Having come naked into the world, he goes out of it naked as well, never having known the joy of living.

Without working, we cannot eat. Without eating, we die. But even if we eat, we die anyway. Without a clear sense of what to do in life, work is meaningless. In fact, more and more people in the process of climbing the corporate ladder have no idea why they are working, and think longingly of leaving their jobs.

Any worker with a clear-cut vision of the purpose of life would be filled with enthusiasm for work—would, as Nietzsche said, desire even suffering, and seek it out. The best stimulant to increase the will to work is a purpose in life.

THE PURPOSE OF IT ALL

Knowing that something good will come of your efforts—that your family will respect and appreciate you more, for example—can make a tough job easier to bear, by investing it with meaning.

However, as global competition makes business and industry increasingly cutthroat and cost-conscious, there is no longer any guarantee that mere diligence will be rewarded. Dog-eat-dog competition is fast becoming the rule of the day. When it is time to retrench, companies are sometimes forced to let go of even highly skilled, long-time workers. Even though a man may have put in twenty or thirty years of his life, even though he may have children's college tuition payments, a mortgage, and elderly parents' looming medical expenses to deal with, he finds himself out of a job. Tragedies like this are now commonplace. Work can be equated with happiness only so long as it is going well. Work-driven people lose their bearings when their work hits a wall. "Take away my position, and what's left of me?" they wail. "What am I to live for?" People who realize only in their twilight years that they lack any system of support may find that it is too late.

In the 2002 movie *About Schmidt*, the title character, who is recently retired and widowed, looks back over his life and says, in voiceover:

> I know we are all pretty small in the big scheme of things. And I suppose the most you can hope for is to make some kind of difference. But what kind of difference have I made? What in the world is better because of me? … I am weak, and I am a failure. There's just no getting around it. Relatively soon, I will die. Maybe in twenty years, maybe tomorrow. It doesn't matter. Once I am dead and everyone who knew me dies too, it will be as though I never even existed. What difference has my life made to anyone? None that I can think of. None at all.

Like many American men, the title character in this movie feels the questions of the meaning and purpose of life weighing heavily on him after retirement.

"Midway in the journey of our life I found myself in a dark wood, for the straight way was lost"[24]: so begins *The Divine Comedy* of Dante. In the same way, there comes a time for everyone when the lies and deception of the world are unbearable, and all seems empty and vain. After a lifetime of dedicated work in the hope of a generous pension, many a hapless worker has reached retirement age only to find, aghast, that his hopes were misplaced. He may turn to his wife for comfort, only to find she has betrayed him or lost interest. His children want nothing more to do with him. Trusted friends and colleagues drift away. He tries to make it on his own, but then illness renders him immobile. All he has left is a pile of unpaid debts. In short, he faces the grim fact that nothing he ever placed faith in was truly trustworthy; all was a broken reed.

Surely nothing in life is so wretched as the moment when one realizes the futility of all one's efforts, or stands appalled at the massive accumulation of a lifetime of unpardonable sins. The harshness of such a judgment is made worse by the fact that it often comes just as one's last physical strength is ebbing away.

CHAPTER 6

Joy Itself Can Bring Sorrow

THE DEATH OF A BELOVED WIFE

The joy shared by two people who fulfill one another's deepest needs is incomparable, a far remove from mere physical attraction or pleasure of the moment. Some of the greatest love songs of our day express this state so well that they are performed over and over by various artists, like "Can't Help Falling in Love"—sung by Elvis Presley: "Like a river flows surely to the sea / Darling so it goes some things are meant to be / Take my hand, take my whole life too / For I can't help falling in love with you."[25] Timeless love songs of this kind express the crux of longing and love so sweetly and succinctly that they are embraced by generations of listeners.

Yet, as we all know, it often happens that intense rapture ends badly. *Romeo and Juliet* contains these cautionary words:

> These violent delights have violent ends
> And in their triumph die, like fire and powder,
> Which as they kiss consume.[26]

In the wedding ceremony, lovers pledge unswerving devotion "till death do us part." Whether death comes early or late, for any who love the one who departs, it is always too soon.

In 1999, Japanese intellectual Jun Eto took his own life, at the age of sixty-six. In a memoir called *My Wife and I*, written three months after losing his beloved wife to illness, he recounts her death in searing words of longing and despair. The book is in fact his own last testament. During his wife's illness, supporting her to the end without leaving her side became his all-consuming goal and the focus of his existence. After her death, he was bereft of any reason for living, left to face a meaningless expanse of time in which to wait for his own death.

The couple had been so close that they were sometimes likened to identical twins. The death of his wife spelled the end of everything. In the book he portrays an almost unbearable longing.

> She murmured to no one in particular, "My life is over now. It's all finished."
>
> There was an echo of such profound desolation in her voice that I could make no reply. It came home to me then that everything was finished for me, too, and that there was nothing I could do about it … Perhaps the medicine had brought her some relief, for she smiled peacefully, looked at me, and said, "We visited a lot of places together, didn't we?" … "We certainly did," I said. "And each one was special in its own way." I could not bring myself to say the words, "We'll go again." Instead, tears running down my cheeks, I retreated into the kitchenette …
>
> As long as my wife's life was not yet exhausted, down to the very last moment I had the clear goal of staying with her, and never leaving her alone; now that she is gone, I have no such goal. I am only obsessed body and soul with the coming hour of my own solitary death, propelled second by second towards a meaningless death.[27]

Why is parting inevitable? Why are we doomed to vanish in the end? Swiss philosopher Karl Hilty (1833–1909) warned that love is "happiness that penetrates the depths of the heart, but it can also become an all-destroying unhappiness … The deeper and purer the emotion of one given over completely to the happiness of love, the more certain that person is to become completely miserable, unless he can escape such a bitter experience through death."[28]

Bliss and suffering, it seems, always go hand in hand. He who seeks joy that mounts to the skies must be prepared to face sorrow unto death.

THE UNDERPINNINGS OF HAPPINESS

In *The Sorrows of Young Werther*, Goethe laments, "Must it ever be thus,—that the source of our happiness must also be the fountain of our misery?"[29]

The very things that contribute most to human happiness—love, health, possessions, fame—are also the cause of unhappiness and tears. That is because the moment these underpinnings are taken away, our happiness crumbles and we cannot help sinking into sorrow.

The great Impressionist painter Pierre-Auguste Renoir (1841–1919) suffered in his declining years from crippling arthritis. Even so, he continued doggedly to paint by holding the brush in his twisted fingers and wrapping it in place with a long bandage. In a letter to a friend dated 1919, he expressed the frustration of not being able to use his talent: "Now that I can no longer count on my arms and legs, I would like to paint large canvases. I dream only of Veronese, of his *Marriage at Cana*. What misery!"[30]

He who gasps for breath in the struggle against illness has lost the prop of health, and he who weeps for a lost love has experienced betrayal. Those who grieve for a dead spouse or child have lost the light of life and are plunged into a vale of tears. From the moment we lay claim to happiness, the hand of misery draws close. Happiness of any kind forsakes us in the end.

Is there no end to this wretchedness but the grave?

THE STING OF MEMORY

"When it's over, it's over. At least I'll have my memories." Some people comfort themselves with this thought. Truthfully, there is no use in mourning lost happiness. The desire to escape present pain by losing oneself in happy memories is universal—but does it actually work? After one has fallen ill, for example, do memories of yesterday's glowing health bring cheer, or simply remind one of what has been lost?

The well-known Beatles song "Yesterday" expresses the predicament very well: "Yesterday, all my troubles seemed so far away / Now it looks as though they're here to stay / Oh, I believe in yesterday / Suddenly, I'm not half the man I used to be / There's a shadow hanging over me / Oh, yesterday came suddenly."[31] No matter how lovely the past may have been, it will never return, and the present is not what we wish it to be. Memories can be sweet, but they do not have power to change our current circumstances.

Not only that, the experience of once-in-a-lifetime happiness can cast a pall over the remainder of one's days. Imagine the feelings of someone suddenly separated forever from a soulmate. This person would likely feel keen regret: "What I believed was my greatest happiness was really my greatest misfortune: Had I never known that happiness, I would be better off today." A taste of grand, radiant happiness makes it hard to settle later for ordinary scraps. Encountering the perfect mate cannot be termed unqualified good fortune.

"There is no greater sorrow than to recall, in wretchedness, the happy time." These words are from Dante's *Inferno*.[32] A too-happy past can serve only to increase the hellish torments of the present.

THE SEARCH FOR A LASTING HAPPINESS

A boy shattered by the death of his beloved dog took to carrying around a stuffed toy squirrel. He explained it this way: "Stuffed animals are better than pets. They're nice, and they don't betray you … Dying is a kind of betrayal."[33]

After the last child marries and moves away, many parents—particularly women, who are often primary caregivers—succumb to a depression that has been named "empty nest syndrome." The reason for this widespread phenomenon is doubtless that to a mother, her children are her very life. Yet the newspapers are full of incidents of children shooting, stabbing, or bludgeoning their parents, often for the most trivial of reasons. It is hard to even imagine the feelings of betrayal and anguish that a parent attacked this way by a child must feel.

In the words of Shakespeare, "How sharper than a serpent's tooth it is / To have a thankless child."[34]

Is there anything that we can devote our whole lives to without regret, besides a lasting happiness with no shadow of betrayal? In this world where everything perishes, imperishable happiness is above all else our common desire, and its attainment is our life's true purpose.

CHAPTER 7

Satisfaction Just Beyond Reach

GOALS ACCOMPLISHED

In his *Symposium*, Plato argues that all humans are born for one purpose only: to search for eternal happiness.[35] Told that humanity shares the universal purpose of finding lasting happiness, some may protest that each individual has a unique purpose in life. This assumption is natural, since individuality and diversity are widely-held core values; each person shines out, then, precisely because he or she is unlike anyone else.

The sorts of goals people usually have in mind are things like getting accepted into college, mastering a foreign language, winning an athletic tournament, having a successful romantic relationship, getting a steady job, building a house, getting rich, winning a Nobel Prize. But these are in fact mere way stations in life, goals that are only relevant for the time being and that bear no resemblance to a true life purpose. "Ace the exam" turns into "land the job," which gives way in turn to "time to buy a house." It is important to establish the difference between ever-changing life goals and an unswerving purpose that explains what we were born to do.

An anonymous samurai penned this wry poem:

> Up close
> it's not so much—
> Mount Fuji

A mountain that from a distance appears majestic can turn out on closer inspection to present an incongruous array of trash and empty soda cans. Goals that we set for ourselves may likewise seem wonderful from a distance, yet let us down in our very moment of triumph. Who has not experienced having a dream come true, only to experience a nagging disappointment: "Is this all?" Ironically, the bigger the goal and the harder one has worked to realize it, the greater the letdown: "What have I been doing all this time? Is this what I sacrificed for? Shouldn't there be something more?"

As Goethe wrote in *Faust*, "Man errs, till he has ceased to strive."[36]

As long as one is alive, one must suffer. No matter how successful we are in school or in business, no matter how much money we may amass or how fine a home we may build, the attainment of goals like these cannot truly satisfy in the end.

WINS ACHIEVED

In 1992, Japanese boxer Katsuya Onizuka became junior bantamweight champion of the world. Though he reached the pinnacle of his sport and even went on to defend his crown, a sense of lasting fulfillment eluded him. Onizuka confesses that his life was an endless cycle of seeking and failing to find what he was looking for.

> When I was a kid, I thought a world boxing champion was like Superman. Next thing to God. If an ordinary Joe like me could ever climb that high, how great a human being would I be? That single thought is what kept me going.
>
> But then when I won, it was nothing like what I expected. "You mean this is it?" I'd think. "How come I don't get anything out of it?" I'd tell myself, "Surely the next time, it'll be different. I'll gain something." Hoping against hope, I went on fighting, match after match—but nothing ever changed.
>
> The night after a match, it drove me crazy to think I had survived yet again without finding what I was looking for. I wanted to jump for joy, but I only felt more and more unfulfilled and frustrated. The same thing happened over and over, up to and including my very last fight.[37]

Alfie Kohn, a U.S. researcher noted for his studies on the ill effects of competition, has discovered that even after attaining a major goal, many athletes are deeply scarred by a sense of futility and disillusionment. He concludes, "Winning fails to satisfy us in any significant way and thus cannot begin to compensate for the pain of losing."[38] Psychiatrist Harvey Ruben concurs, noting that "the discovery … that 'making it' is often a hollow gain is one of the most traumatic events that the successful competitor can experience."[39] An infinite distance separates the reality of success from the success of our imagination.

THE ACCUMULATION OF WEALTH

The same thing can be seen in the world of business. In his book *Meaning in Life: The Creation of Value*, MIT professor of philosophy Irving Singer observes that for many people, work that is going well can suddenly seem stupid and pointless: "People who devote themselves to a worthy but stultifying career toward which their upbringing has steered them may suddenly feel that everything they do is meaningless. This can happen to virtually anyone."[40]

The decade of the 1980s was a time of unabashed desire for wealth in the U.S. Billionaires were written up as heroes in popular magazines, and became the focus of national attention. But life at the top is not easy; it is far easier to climb up to a mountain peak than it is to stay there long. Sooner or later, the question arises: "What's the use of all this money?" Does anyone ever wish on their deathbed that they'd spent their life making more money?

Billionaire real estate developer Donald Trump, one of the world's richest men, confesses that he, too, feels this way:

> It's a rare person who can achieve a major goal in life and not almost immediately start feeling sad, empty, and a little lost … Actually, I don't have to look at anyone else's life to know that's true. I'm as susceptible to that pitfall as anyone else.[41]

Without a proper understanding of the purpose of life, all the wealth, possessions and fame in the world, gained at whatever peril of mortal combat or arduous labor, would seem meaningless.

A PURPOSE THAT NEVER FADES

The satisfaction of achieving our goals is short-lived, fading before long to a mere memory. The satisfaction of realizing life's purpose, however, is utterly different: it neither withers nor fades. As we saw in the previous chapter, our ultimate aim is to achieve lasting happiness. No achievement that quickly turns hollow, or that is reduced to a mere memory, can possibly be called the true *purpose of life*.

And yet many people are without hope, convinced that lasting happiness is unobtainable.

What sort of life is it, spent pursuing goals that provide only a fleeting sense of satisfaction? Your sense of achievement on attaining a goal soon disintegrates, putting you back at the starting line. This time things will be different, you think, and apply yourself with redoubled energy—but all you do is go round in circles, never feeling the joy in life that exults, "How glad I am to have been born human!" True joy in life lies forever out of reach. What could be more tragic than this?

In the words of nineteenth-century German philosopher Schopenhauer, the thankless life "swings like a pendulum to and fro between pain and boredom." [42]

We fight for prizes of dubious value—"even for an eggshell" [43]—deceived by hopes that "over the mountains lives Happiness," [44] and then, having found no deep-seated satisfaction or peace of mind, we fall at last into the arms of death. If that is all life is, why then is each human life so infinitely precious?

CHAPTER 8

The Vast Immovable Wall of Death

The Tale of the Heike, a medieval cycle of stories set in the latter half of the twelfth century, has been described by Edward Seidensticker as an "admirable parable upon the evanescence of things." The message of its opening line reverberates through the text and across the centuries: "The bell of the Gion Temple tolls into every man's heart to warn him that all is vanity and evanescence."[45]

The realities that we cling to—health, possessions, reputation, home—are in constant flux. The change from moment to moment may be large or miniscule, but it leads inexorably to destruction.

> Life changes fast.
> Life changes in the instant.
> You sit down to dinner and life as you know it ends.[46]

In her bestselling nonfiction work *The Year of Magical Thinking,* author Joan Didion explains that on the evening of December 30, 2003, just after they sat down to dinner, her husband had "a sudden massive coronary event that caused his death." It happened at the end of a perfectly ordinary day, a day like any other. Her husband was sipping a Scotch and talking with her. All of a sudden she looked up to find him slumped motionless, with his left hand in the air. Thinking that it was some kind of a joke, she said, "Don't do that." But her husband never responded to her again.[47]

The death of a loved one is shocking; but hardest of all to accept is the inevitability of one's own death. Just after his retirement, Wataru Hiromatsu (1933–94), professor of philosophy at the University of Tokyo, was suddenly felled by cancer. A giant in Japanese academic circles, he was thoroughly versed not only in philosophy but in science, psychology, economics, sociology, history, and other fields as well. Of his lifework, a projected three-volume study titled *Being and Meaning*, only the first half ever reached publication. In his introduction to Volume II—which would be his final work—he touched on his plans for the rest, ending with the plaintive inscription, "O for ordinary, peaceful days!"

I can't die now! Or so we think—but Death has other plans.

Hideo Kishimoto (1903–64), a professor of religion at the University of Tokyo who lost a long battle against cancer, left an account of his struggle against the disease in which he likened death to sudden, unprovoked violence.

> Death always comes suddenly. No matter when it appears, the one visited by Death looks on its arrival as a sudden intrusion. For the mind filled with a sense of security is totally unprepared for Death … Death comes when by rights it has no business coming. It goes coolly where by rights it has no business going, like a desperado striding with dirty boots into a freshly cleaned parlor. Death's behavior is outrageous. You may ask it to wait awhile, but in vain. Death is a monster beyond human power to budge or to hold in check.[48]

Any outcome we construct, by whatever hardships and toil, will be quashed in the final act of life as the curtain comes crashing down. It is exactly like blowing bubbles; however giant a bubble you may contrive to blow, it is destined to burst in the end.

At the end of his masterwork *Being and Nothingness*, French existential philosopher Jean-Paul Sartre wrote, "Man is a useless passion."[49] What is so wretched as a life spent in pursuit of things destined to come to nothing? Why do people slave away with their eyes fixed on the here and now?

THE LONGING FOR MEANING

Nietzsche wrote in *Thus Spake Zarathustra*, "As deeply as man looketh into life, so deeply also doth he look into suffering."[50] The more we try to think whether in life there is anything truly worth seeking, the more it often seems that all is meaningless.

Some would argue, "Love and accept life in all its meaninglessness." In answer to the question "Why do we live," Shinji Miyadai, an outspoken and controversial associate professor of sociology at Tokyo Metropolitan University, made this assertion: "Life has no meaning whatever, and there is no compelling reason to live."[51] A young admirer of Miyadai's works subsequently killed himself, as did a female college student in one of the professor's classes. Miyadai reflected back on the first incident: "At the risk of being misunderstood, let me say it could be argued that S was 'killed' by my insensitivity."[52] Concerning the young woman's death, he wrote that his words had apparently "functioned in the end to heighten her sense of meaninglessness."[53] Enraged by the professor's irresponsibility in making such statements around impressionable young people and robbing them of their will to live, a group of readers collaborated to produce a book of protest entitled *Down With Shinji Miyadai!*

If we follow Miyadai's advice and avoid struggling with hard questions about why we live or what we are to do with our lives, and instead drift carelessly along at the mercy of external phenomena, it may not matter much whether we live to be eighty or die now. Miyadai himself seems to have realized this, confessing himself incapable of drifting: "In my writings I advise people to 'be laid-back about life,' but I myself am not at all laid-back, as [young people] are. I could never live in such a way."[54]

Twentieth-century French writer Albert Camus said that deep in the human heart is a "wild longing" to know the meaning of life.[55] We want to know, indeed we must know the meaning of life if we are to go on living. That is how we humans are made.

Anyone who insists that he or she can get along without a purpose in life is neither happy nor unhappy. Probably such a person is merely preoccupied.

THE WHISPER DEEP IN THE SOUL

After the devastating Great Hanshin Earthquake of 1995 reduced the streets of Kobe to rubble, rescue squads and volunteer groups carried out desperately needed relief work at the risk of their own lives. One sixty-seven-year-old man who narrowly escaped death was rescued with tears of joy and cries of elation, only to end his life later in despair, after coming to regret that he had not died in the quake. While living in prefab emergency shelter for survivors, he had often been heard to grumble, "What am I doing here? How long must I go on like this?" He was by no means the only survivor of the quake to decide on suicide. When we run headlong into a wall of misfortune and unhappiness, the question "Why live?" comes sharply into focus.

An essay in a corporate publication titled "What Is the Purpose of Life?" contains a description of the mixed emotions the author feels on receiving the kind of New Year's greetings that contain letters outlining the milestone events that occurred in the sender's life over the past year:

> It is certainly true that obtaining a license, taking lessons, and being healthy can all be important factors contributing to a richer life. I understand, I do, and yet I cannot help wondering—do these people not hear the whisper deep in the soul that says, "You are going to die. One of these days, you will die"? … The children's school expenses need to be paid, I need to make a decent living, I want to play some golf, or go out drinking or take a trip now and then as a matter of pride. I fear that I myself will go on using excuses like these to put off consideration of the purpose of life, right up until the day I die.[56]

Preoccupations like the children's schooling or leisure-time pursuits like golf or travel cannot stop anxiety from growing: "With death around the corner, what am I doing, devoting myself to this? What if I die without ever having confronted the meaning of life?" A decayed tooth that causes an occasional twinge in the early stages will, left untreated, end in sleepless agony.

Our lives are a constant search for happiness, yet we are in a headlong rush toward the one place we fear most—the grave. There is no greater contradiction than this. Those who live only for the sake of living are, in a real sense, living with death as their goal. Although they may try to silence them, they hear the whispers deep within: "At the moment of death, all is lost. Yet somewhere, effort must have its reward!" "What if death comes suddenly, before I have time to prepare?" "What should I be doing now?"

When we look straight at the future that awaits us beyond all doubting, we find ourselves face to face with life's greatest issue.

NAKED ANXIETY

We are in the midst of a health boom that borders on the excessive. Television shows and magazine articles are full of information on everything from diets that promote health to the safety of genetically altered foods and concerns about pollution from environmental hormones. Colds rouse barely a ripple of attention, but the words "cancer" and "AIDS" are red flags. That is because they represent diseases that are often fatal.

The German-born philosopher Paul Tillich (1886–1965) wrote in *The Courage to Be* that human beings cannot bear even for an instant the "naked anxiety" of death.[57] A straight-on confrontation with death itself would be too terrifying, and so instead we battle illness and environmental problems. Fear of nuclear war, or earthquakes, or depression, is based ultimately on the threat of death.

Each of us is "Death's fool."[58] Struggle to escape as we will, we can only run full tilt toward death. What may lie beyond the wall of death, we cannot say.

Is there any anxiety greater than an uncertain future? Because we are running in the dark, nothing we may happen to pick up along the way can provide heartfelt cheer. What is the source of this suffering, we ask. Unless we know the true cause of life's suffering, we can never know true relief or contentment. The ultimate purpose of life is to have the root of all suffering eliminated and be filled with the joy that exults, "How glad I am to have been born human!"

Confronting death does not mean sliding vainly into depression; rather, it is the first step toward making the moments of our life outshine the sun.

KNOW THE ROOT OF SUFFERING

To the person thinking seriously about life, advice to "find your passion and follow it" is not helpful. Certainly, absorbing oneself in sports or business can be deeply satisfying and make us feel that this is why we are alive—but only for as long as we forget the shadow of death. Once that whisper in the center of our being starts up ("One day you will die"), then even in the midst of a favorite activity, even after achieving a cherished goal, deep-seated anxieties reassert themselves: "My dreams may have come true, but still, I feel empty." "Why is happiness always mixed with sadness?" "A brief blaze, hastily snuffed—every experience I ever had came down to this." "Is there anything—a purpose in life— that can truly satisfy the soul?"

No one grappling with doubts like these can be satisfied with advice to find his or her own meaning in life. The suggestion that people's purposes in life all differ ignores the universal problem of death, which is why it lacks the power to resolve basic human distress.

Look death squarely in the face, know the root of suffering, and see it eliminated. Only then will the purpose of life become clear. "How wonderful it is to be alive!" you will declare, and marvel, "So this is why we live, to gain supreme happiness!"

THE ULTIMATE PURPOSE OF LIFE

As mentioned above, underlying Plato's *Symposium* is the idea that eternal happiness is the universal purpose of life. Once we have grasped the purpose of life, we gain the ability to distinguish eternal happiness from happiness that wears thin and fades, and true purpose in life from temporary goals and consolations. Since most philosophies of life fail to distinguish between goals in life and the ultimate purpose of life, it is not always easy to tell them apart.

Shinran separated the two clearly, setting forth the purpose of life with unmistakable clarity. In his masterwork *Teaching, Practice, Faith, Enlightenment*, he declared, "Not knowing what is true and what is provisional causes people to miss the great benefit of Amida's compassion."[59] This means, "Those who cannot tell the difference between the true (life's true purpose) and the provisional (human relationships, pastimes, and temporal goals) do not know the ultimate purpose of life, and so miss out on the joy in living that rejoices, 'How wonderful that I was born human!'"

Once we achieve the true purpose of life, all suffering is repaid. Every tear shed comes back to us a pearl.

What is the nature of the eternal happiness awaiting us? We will take up that question in detail in the next section.

Part Two

The Words of Shinran

THE LIFE OF SHINRAN

1173   Born in Kyoto

age 9   Enters the Buddhist priesthood

age 29   Achieves life's purpose through the Vow of Amida

age 31   Breaks ancient taboos by eating fish and taking a wife

age 35   Banished to the province of Echigo (Niigata Prefecture)

age 60+ Returns to Kyoto

age 90   Dies in Kyoto

See Chapter 28 for further details on the life of Shinran.

   Please note that throughout this book, Shinran's age is given following the traditional Japanese way of reckoning, to conform with established precedent.

CHAPTER 1

The Eternal Questions

What do people live for?

This ancient, ever-new question was debated some twenty-four hundred years ago in Greece, as recorded in Plato's *Gorgias* dialogue. Callicles proposed that the proper way for a man to live is to allow his desires to expand without limit, and to devise means to satisfy all his longings.

Today's residents of advanced industrial nations would appear to be true followers and devotees of Callicles. From the time of the industrial revolution in the eighteenth century, when products were first manufactured by machine, it is fair to say that people's efforts and ingenuity have been increasingly focused on how to get all the things they want—how to gratify their desires with maximum efficiency.

Twentieth-century humanity in particular, confident that material affluence was the key to happiness, began to glorify material prosperity. At the same time, people's desires have continually inflated. As society prospers and produces more and more goods, consumers come to want more and more, from personal computers to flat-screen TVs to new cars. American economist John Kenneth Galbraith (1908–2006), author of *The Affluent Society*, termed this the "dependence effect."

One of the latest scientific marvels has made it possible to talk to virtually anyone, anywhere, while walking down the street. Now that even primary schoolchildren hold cell phones to their ears, it is hard to remember back not so long ago when few in Japan could afford even a wristwatch. Microwave cooking has vastly simplified meal preparation. Ubiquitous ATMs have made cash deposits and withdrawals possible 24/7, while thanks to Internet banking, you can check your balance and transfer funds in the convenience and privacy of your own home. A particularly wonderful recent invention is a camera tiny enough to swallow that can transmit live images of the entire digestive tract from inside the body.

The world has definitely become a more convenient place—so why do we not have a lasting sense of happiness? We may obtain things we want, one after another, yet we can never keep up with our galloping desires; instead, we feel unsatisfied and empty.

Suicides are on the increase in developed nations, along with bizarre crimes and tragic accidents. In Japan, a nine-year-old girl was kidnapped and imprisoned in a young man's room for nine years, until she was eighteen, in what is surely one of the most fiendish incidents in the annals of modern crime. When her captor tortured her with a stun gun or physical blows, ordering her to keep silent, she bit down on her arms or a blanket to keep from crying out.

The year 2000 saw a surge in juvenile crime as well. A boy murdered a housewife, and then bragged that he had done it just to find out what killing was like. Hearing this story, a seventeen-year-old annoyed that the other boy "beat me to it" promptly went out and hijacked a bus, cruelly slitting the throat of one passenger and wounding five others. He put the passengers through fifteen hours of unremitting terror, and after he was apprehended, declared brazenly, "Who says I did anything bad?" A fifteen-year-old planning to murder the entire family of a friend stabbed three people to death with a survival knife, and gravely wounded the remaining three. Stories like these simply leave one speechless.

EINSTEIN'S DECLARATION

Despite material gains of recent times and the vastly changed lifestyles we enjoy today, happiness does not lie that way. Throughout the twentieth century, science made rapid strides, becoming the most powerful tool in history, and yet was used to carry out unprecedented mass murders and ultimately to threaten the destruction of the human race itself.

Albert Einstein declared that it is the role of religion to teach the ends for which science ought to be used. In *The World As I See It*, he wrote, "What is the meaning of human life … ? To answer this question at all implies a religion."[60] The twenty-first century has been labeled by some the "age of religion," because people are in search of a true religion that can pinpoint the ultimate meaning of life.

Does human life have a purpose?
"Yes, achieve it quickly!"

This was the sole message preached by Shinran. It was he who set forth clearly the purpose of life—humanity's cardinal concern. Anyone who learns this purpose as he laid it out will understand why the life and teachings of Shinran continue to move and inspire so many people.

Throughout Part Two of this book, we will demonstrate how the words of Shinran show what it is that we live for.

CHAPTER 2

Shinran's Answer

THE GREAT SHIP OF AMIDA'S VOW

Why are we born, and why do we live? Why is it wrong to take one's own life, even amid great pain? What is the ultimate purpose of life?

With unswerving conviction and courage, Shinran gave an answer that is brief and brilliant: *There is a great ship that will bear us cheerfully across life's sea of ceaseless suffering, and our mission is to board this ship and live in eternal happiness.*

The introduction to *Teaching, Practice, Faith, Enlightenment*,[61] Shinran's most important work, begins with these lines:

> Amida's inconceivable Vow is a great ship that carries us across the sea that is difficult to cross, and his unimpeded light is the sun of wisdom that destroys the mind of darkness.[62]

This is a great manifesto for all humanity. It means that Amida's Vow to save all beings is the sun that eradicates the darkness which is the root of human suffering, and a great ship on which all are borne cheerfully and happily across life's sea of endless waves of tribulation. To board this ship is indeed the purpose of life.

What does it actually mean to board the great ship that carries us across the sea of suffering? Answering that question is the theme of this book. In a nutshell, it is this: to have one's darkness of mind (the root of suffering) eliminated, and know the joy of life that exults, "How glad I am to have been born human!" Shinran left many writings, but it is fair to say that everything he wrote can be summed up in these words.

WE WERE NOT BORN TO SUFFER

As we have seen already, Shinran compares life to a sea in which human beings suffer wave after wave of distress. He calls this the "sea that is difficult to cross" or the "sea of tribulation."

Before he died, Tokugawa Ieyasu (1542–1616), the powerful warrior chieftain who was awarded the ancient title of *seii taishogun* ("barbarian-subduing generalissimo"), is said to have compared his life to "traveling a long road, laden with a heavy burden." Never once, in other words, was he able to set down the burden of suffering. Even an unparalleled optimist like Goethe lamented in 1824, "The course of my existence … at bottom … has been nothing but pain and burden, and I can affirm that during the whole of my 75 years, I have not had four weeks of genuine well-being." [63]

Similar sentiments have been expressed by some of Japan's finest writers. Fumiko Hayashi (1903–51), known for her free-spirited life, wrote: "The life of the flower is short, and full of suffering." Novelist Soseki Natsume (1867–1916) wrote in a letter to his wife, "Humans may be animals meant to live and suffer." It was the short-story writer and essayist Ryunosuke Akutagawa (1892–1927) who said, "Life is more hellish than Hell." [64] One does not need to listen to these laments to concur with the words of the Buddha, uttered some twenty-six hundred years ago: "Life is suffering."

Yet we were not born to suffer; that is not why we live. The ultimate wish of every person is the same: to do away with suffering and cross life's sea of tribulation with all cheer and happiness. This is the greatest challenge of mankind, and the solution lies in Shinran's magnum opus, *Teaching, Practice, Faith, Enlightenment.*

CHAPTER 3

The Root Cause of Suffering

Why do people suffer?

An animal that is struck will yelp in pain and run away, but human beings insist on knowing the reason for an unpleasant experience, and what they can do to prevent it from happening again. Failure to pin down the cause with accuracy can lead to devastating results, as when curable illnesses prove fatal. Providing appropriate treatment for abdominal pain, for example, depends on knowing whether the source is an ulcer, cancer, nerves, or something else. Without a proper diagnosis, the patient's suffering will not abate. What if, for instance, a case of stomach cancer were treated as an ulcer? The damage would be irreparable, regret never-ending. Identifying the cause of a disease is of the essence in treatment.

In the same way, in order for us to enjoy a life of supreme pleasure, it is essential to examine the reality of the truth that life is suffering, and to identify the root cause of the suffering that permeates our lives. This is humanity's crying need.

Shinran identified the true cause of human suffering in these words:

Circling among the houses of the birth-and-death cycle
Is caused by one thing alone: the doubting mind.[65]

The condition of going around and around in endless circles of torment without satisfaction or rest is referred to as "the birth-and-death cycle" or "the endless wheel of suffering." The condition of endless suffering that we cannot escape is likened to a house apart from which we cannot live.[66]

The great Russian writer Fyodor Dostoevsky (1821–81), from his first-hand experiences in a Siberian labor camp, declared in *Memoirs from the House of the Dead* that the cruelest punishment of all would be to compel someone to do "utterly useless and nonsensical" work.[67] During his imprisonment, he and his fellow convicts did things like bake bricks, paint walls, and plow fields. Even though they were forced to do heavy labor, it was not without purpose, as through their toil the men produced food or built houses. Understanding the purpose of their work made it possible for them to endure the difficult conditions of captivity.

What if work was made punishment? Suppose convicts had to move a large mountain of dirt from point A to point B. Then, once the job was done, suppose the sweating men were ordered to move the mountain back to its original position. And when that was done, to move it back to point B, and so on. What would happen to men condemned to that sort of meaningless, pointless labor? It would cause a man to "hang himself after a few days," as Dostoevsky wrote, or else to go mad, bash his head against a stone, and die. This is the punishment of "never-ending suffering."

But in fact, is not life a great deal like this?

> When at last I came
> to the peak that I had thought
> would surely be the last,
> I turned my eyes to the way beyond—
> mountain piled on mountain.
>   —Anonymous

Sickness, the death of a relative or loved one, a sudden accident, conflicts at home and at work, disputes with neighbors, examinations, competition, sudden layoffs, heavy debt, apprehension about old age: just as one difficulty is overcome, before one can relax, the next appears.

THE ROOT CAUSE OF SUFFERING 55

According to tradition, the souls of dead children are sent to the banks of "Sai no Kawara," the dry bed of the river of souls, where they pile pebbles into small towers in an attempt to distract themselves from their suffering. A demon soon comes along and scatters the stones, forcing the children to start all over again. In the same way, everything that we, the living, painstakingly build up with sweat and tears is apt to collapse before our eyes in a second. "I can't believe this is happening to me!" How many times have we said those words, full of amazement or chagrin or regret at some unforeseen disaster?

> Over this hill, happiness lies waiting:
> clinging to that hope,
> seven hills have I crossed so far,
> this my fortieth year.[68]

These lines from a popular song struck a chord with the Japanese public precisely because everyone has experienced something like that. In hopes of attaining happiness, we scramble for dear life up the mountain in front of us, only to find a still steeper slope waiting on the other side. Tottering, we pull ourselves together and puff our way up again, thinking surely *this* will be the last one. Is not life a succession of such experiences? That is what Shinran meant by "circling among the houses of the birth-and-death cycle."

HAVING AND NOT-HAVING

Floating up from the waves of life's sea of suffering are cries like these:
"If only I had more money!"
"If only I had possessions!"
"If only I were famous!"
"If only I had more status!"
"If only I had my own home!"
"If only I had a sweetheart!"
And so on and so on. Believing that their suffering derives from some such lack, people set their sights on a nearby log or plank and swim for it with all their might—but will that get them across the sea?

The following anecdote may give food for thought. In a tropical country, an American was scolding a man dozing under a palm tree. "Why don't you stop being so lazy? Get a job and make yourself some money!"

The man looked up and said, "What do I need to make money for?"

"Save it in the bank and before you know it, you'll have a big pile."

"What would I do with a big pile of money?"

"You could build a big house. Then if you made more money, you could build a villa where it is warm."

"What would I do with a villa?"

"You could go out in the garden and take a nap under a palm tree."

"I already *am* taking a nap under a palm tree!"

Such shallow visions of happiness are destined to come to nothing, as we can see all around us.

If, as many people assume, suffering can be attributed to a lack of money, things, reputation, or status, then someone blessed with all of that should enjoy a blissful existence. But is that so? History is full of examples proving otherwise; we need not look far to find many pitiable cases. Princess Diana, the flower of the British royal family, is said to have attempted suicide five times. She had beauty, prestige, wealth, an enviable marriage that was once called "the match of the century"—yet privately she bore inexpressible sorrow.

Yasunari Kawabata, author of *Snow Country* and the recipient of Japan's first Nobel Prize for literature in 1968, gassed himself to death. Despite his genius and accolades, he too was a man of many sorrows.

American Wallace H. Carothers (1896–1937) invented nylon, which was soon used to produce stockings of dramatic resiliency. His employers at DuPont reportedly rewarded their brilliant chemist with exceptional treatment. For the rest of his life, wherever he traveled and whatever five-star restaurant he chose to eat in, the company agreed to shoulder the cost. Paying for a lifetime of travel and gastronomy must have seemed well worth the cost if it meant keeping their star employee happy. Yet Carothers committed suicide at forty-one.

If money, talent, honor, and status were enough to eliminate suffering, surely these three would not have seen fit to commit or attempt suicide. The Larger Sutra of Infinite Life states:

> He who has no field is distressed and wishes for one; he who has no house is distressed and wishes for one. He who owns a field is distressed about the field, and he who owns a house is distressed about the house. It is no different with horses and other livestock, servants, money and treasure, food and clothing, and household goods: having and not-having are the same.

A person who lacks a field or house must trouble himself about seeking one out, and a person who owns land and houses must trouble himself with their management and upkeep. The same principle applies to all kinds of possessions: if we lack them we fret, and if we have them we suffer on their account. Haves are bound with chains of gold, have-nots with chains of iron. Whatever the chains are made of, the suffering they cause is equally real.

Śākyamuni Buddha taught that "having and not-having are the same": in either state, our inability to escape from suffering is unchanged.

Whatever possessions and power we may obtain—even if we rocket off to outer space—unless we face the root cause of suffering, and unless this cause is eradicated, we can never set down life's burdens.

CHAPTER 4

The Dark Mind: The Source of Suffering

THE WORDS OF SHINRAN

What is the root of human suffering? As we have seen, Shinran's answer in *Teaching, Practice, Faith, Enlightenment* is plain and unequivocal: it "is caused by one thing alone: the doubting mind." The only cause is doubt. Shinran's words are free of tentativeness; as he expounds the sole solution to suffering, such assertions are frequent in his writings. Here "doubt" means the darkness of mind that does not know what will happen after death, concerning which we will have more to say in the following chapters.

Probably no one, on being told that the source of suffering is darkness of mind, will immediately see the light. People are much more likely to show bewilderment, or dismiss the assertion with a careless shrug. Even those who do take a critical look at themselves are likely to feel that their troubles are rooted in worldly passions such as desire, anger, and envy. These passions are known in the teachings of Buddhism as *bonno*, a word written with characters for "trouble" and "distress."

SHINRAN'S YOUTHFUL STRUGGLE WITH WORLDLY PASSIONS

Like the cherry blossom,
the heart planning on tomorrow
is ephemeral indeed—

what sudden storm may not arise
in the middle of the night?

Shinran lost his father at age four and his mother at age eight. Startled
to realize that he would be the next to die, he entered the Buddhist
priesthood at the age of nine, and wrote this poem on that occasion. For
the next twenty years he lived on Mount Hiei in Kyoto, in a monastery
central to Buddhism of that time, engaged in a pitched battle with his
own worldly passions. The following account paints a vivid picture of
his struggle:

> Try as I will to quiet the waters of my heart, the waves of
> thought continually move; try as I will to achieve a mind
> bright as the full moon, clouds of delusion blanket it. If my
> next breath should stop, I would fall into Hell. How can I in-
> dulge myself in trivial socializing and wear myself out with
> useless studies? Swiftly, I must cast aside worldly desires and
> seek liberation.[69]

As he pursued ascetic training on the mountain at night, Shinran could
see Lake Biwa in the distance, reflecting the full moon like a mirror.
"Why cannot my mind be as serene as the water in that lake?" he would
ask himself in deep frustration. "One after another, thoughts I should
not think rise unbidden to the surface of my mind. My heart is aswirl
with ideas I should not entertain. It is too horrible. Why am I a seething
cauldron of anger and desire? I must do something ..."

Reduced to tears by the turmoil of his passion-filled mind, so different from the tranquil lake, Shinran raised his eyes to the sky above,
where the full moon was shining brightly. "Why can I not see the moon
of enlightenment as clearly as I can see the moon in the sky? Foul clouds
befog the sky of my mind. Must I go to my death with a mind so
black?"

Aware that every breath he drew brought him closer to the world of
eternal suffering after death, Shinran became distraught. He thought,
"With this great problem at hand, I have no time to waste. I must cast
aside all earthly desires and quickly find a solution. There is not a second

to spare. Somewhere I must find a great teacher, a priest of true virtue, to show me the way to salvation." The words recorded in the book *Panegyric* convey the anguish Shinran felt on leaving Mount Hiei behind, shedding bitter tears as he made his way down the mountain of so many memories.

Soon afterwards he would meet Honen (1133–1212), the founder of the Pure Land School of Buddhism, who taught him "the Vow of Amida which eliminates the dark mind that is the source of human suffering, and imparts blissful life beyond measure." Shinran's surprise and joy at this encounter and this revelation must have been beyond all imagining.

THE ENCOUNTER WITH HONEN

> To meet with a true master
> is difficult above all else;
> the endless wheel of suffering
> comes only from the doubting mind.[70]

These lines from *Hymns on the Masters* may be paraphrased as, "Oh, how hard it is to find someone who can teach the true message of Buddha—that the source of human suffering is darkness of mind." The words overflow with Shinran's profound delight at meeting Honen and his strong emotion on learning the true cause of suffering.

The word used for "master" here refers specifically to someone who conveys the teachings of Buddha. A "true master" is one who teaches true Buddhism.

What do most Japanese people think of when they hear the word "Buddhism"?

The word calls up various associations. First in most people's minds is "funeral Buddhism," which thrives on funerals, memorial services, and sutra chanting. Next is "invocation Buddhism," dispensing this-worldly favors to worshippers who pay to burn incense or cedar sticks. But that is not all. We could also name "sightseeing Buddhism," which makes money off temple compounds and statues; "business Buddhism," where priests pay more attention to operating various lines of business than to the faith, busying themselves with management of schools, kindergartens and such; "double-duty Buddhism," where priests moonlight as teachers, rent out temple compounds as parking lots, etc.; and finally, "death anniversary Buddhism," which seeks to profit from memorial services marking the deaths of great masters like Shinran and Rennyo (1415–99; a descendant of Shinran's who brought about a revival of the True Pure Land School or Shin Buddhism). Of course, none of these enterprises comes close to approximating the true nature of Buddhism.

All too often, those monks who do speak of Buddhism mistakenly teach that worldly passions like desire, anger, and envy are the source of suffering, and offer advice on how to overcome them. To meet with a true master—one who teaches that the ultimate root of suffering is darkness of mind—is truly as rare as stars on a rainy night. It is not hard to understand why Shinran wrote with such exultation of his rare good fortune in encountering the priest Honen, who taught him the truth about the "wheel of suffering." How happy he must have been to meet Honen, how thrilled to have his darkness of mind eliminated! Elsewhere in *Hymns on the Masters* he described his reaction in these words:

> Never in all my lives in aeons past
> did I know the strong power for liberation.
> Were it not for the true teacher Genku,[71]
> this life should have ended in vain as well.[72]

This means, "From endless ages past, I knew neither the source of suffering nor the power of Amida's Vow to eradicate it. If I had not met the teacher of true Buddhism, Honen, I would have lost this precious chance as well and suffered eternally after death, never knowing either the purpose of my life or the way to fulfill it. Honen saved me from imminent peril."

What, then, is the nature of the dark mind that is the root of human suffering?

CHAPTER 5

The Mind Shrouded in Ignorance

WE ARE ALL TRAVELERS TOWARD THE WORLD AFTER DEATH

The "dark mind" means the mind shrouded in ignorance of what happens after death.

People often shy from the subject of death as somehow ill-omened, as if to say, "Don't talk about it, or you'll be next to go!" You are as likely to fall dead after talking about death as you are to come into a windfall after talking about money, to be awarded a Nobel Prize after talking about the nominees, or to have a house build itself after you have been talking about a blueprint. The death taboo goes unchallenged, but it is silly.

In the Japanese language, the number four is a homophone for death. As a result, hospital sickrooms have no number four, elevators have no button for the fourth floor, and so on. (A similar phenomenon occurs in the West, where the number thirteen is considered unlucky, and many high-rises have no thirteenth floor.) Such resistance shows the extent of people's fear of the terminal station of life through which all must pass.

> New Year's decorations,
> mileposts on the journey
> to the other world—
> auspicious and not auspicious
> at the same time.

In this poem, the Zen monk Ikkyu (1394–1481) makes the point that human beings are all travelers on a journey to the next world—that is, the world after death. There is no doubting the truth of this observation. Each day that we live brings us one day closer to death. Stopping all the clocks in the world would not stop our progress along that route. This is a stern reality shared by everyone alive. Nobody would knowingly set foot in an aircraft certain to crash, yet from the day of our birth, each of us is a passenger on just such a doomed flight.

THE TIGER IN THE MOUNTAINS

Death is the destiny awaiting us all, and yet few people give it much serious thought. We would rather just not dwell on it. The sudden passing of an acquaintance, a friend, or a relative forces us to stare the unpleasant fact of death in the face, which may cause some to tremble with anxiety and fear; but that is only a temporary state. We soon forget again, filling in the hole in the heart with questions of how best to live. Accepting death's inevitability does not stop us from pushing it into the distant future.

> All this time it was
> only other people who died,
> or so I had assumed—
> now the thought of my own death
> is more than I can bear.

This poem is said to have been written by a physician on his deathbed. The difference between attending other people's deaths and contemplating one's own imminent demise has been likened to the difference between seeing a tiger in a zoo and coming face-to-face with one in the mountains. Even if we tremble with anxiety and fear when someone close to us dies, we are looking at a caged tiger, not at the wild beast loose in the mountains.

But what if you were told that you suffered from terminal cancer and had only one month to live? According to Hideo Kishimoto, the former professor of religion at the University of Tokyo who battled cancer for ten years before passing away, at such a time all else recedes, leaving only the burning question, "What will happen after I die?" Kishimoto's record of his confrontation with death is gripping.

> What does it really mean, the cutting off of life? Certainly it means the end of the physical life of the body. Breathing ceases, the heart comes to a stop ... But human life is not constituted only by the physiological body. At least while a person is alive, it is common sense to think of him or her as a spiritual entity as well. In the now of life, one has a consciousness of self. There is someone whom one knows as "oneself." Matters quickly focus, therefore, on the point of what will become of "oneself" after death. This is the great question for all human beings.[73]

COMFORTING THE DEAD

Even people who deny that there is life after death often change their mind on the death of a friend or acquaintance. They may speak of the "spirit of the departed," or offer prayers for the repose of the loved one's soul. In Japan, the set expression *gomeifuku o inorimasu* is specifically a prayer for happiness in the other world, obviously based on the assumption that such a world does exist. Set expressions directed through tears to the deceased include *yasuraka ni onemuri kudasai* ("Sleep in peace") and *mayowazu ni jobutsu shite kudasai* ("Attain Buddhahood straight away"). After a shipwreck or other disaster at sea, it is common for bereaved people to go to the accident site to throw out flowers or other tokens from a plane or boat. This is no empty ritual. Mourners' faces are solemn, their gestures circumspect.

Every August, Japan remembers its war dead with memorial services called *ireisai*, literally "soul-comforting ceremonies." Without the assumption that souls of the dead exist and need comforting, ceremonies like this would never take place. In the natural order of things, one does not offer comfort to someone who is happy, as there is no need to do so.

Yet many Japanese continue praying for the happiness of souls in the next world while denying the existence of an afterlife; something keeps them from acting in accord with their denials.

Such actions can be laughed off as social niceties only by those still fortunate enough never to have experienced the death of a relative. Sooner or later, death forces itself on the attention. Some protest, "You will never know what happens after death until you die anyway, so the subject is not worth discussing"—yet those same people think nothing of planning against fires and saving for old age without knowing whether they will ever experience either contingency. In fact, most of us will never be in a fire, and anyone who dies young need not worry about old age, and yet—"just in case"—people go on assiduously taking out fire insurance and saving for a rainy day. Nobody says, "You will never know what old age is like until you are old anyway, so who cares?" The inconsistency of taking seriously the possibility of fires and old age while ignoring the absolute certainty of death seems not to occur to anyone.

Excuses abound. "Thinking about it will not change anything." "I'll worry about it when the time comes—if I spent my time thinking about that now, I could not live my life!" Something in death makes people stubbornly avert their eyes, as if facing up to its inevitability would compel a drastic choice between unconditional surrender and last-ditch resistance.

As long as one's health remains good, it is possible to adopt the easygoing view of death as "repose" or "eternal sleep," and claim not to find it menacing at all; in the clutch moment of one's own imminent demise, however, all that matters is what lies beyond death's curtain. In life we contemplate the absolutely unknown "after death," uncertain whether there is any such thing, or any reason for hope. This state alone—the state of ignorance and anxiety about what will become of one after death—is called the "mind of darkness" or "dark mind." Darkness here refers to human ignorance or uncertainty about what will happen after death.

CHAPTER 6

The Dark Future Casts a Shadow on the Present

Many readers may wonder how the dark mind uncertain about what lies beyond death could be the root cause of suffering in life. But what happens when the future is shadowy? To gain some insight, think of these examples: an important exam looming three days off weighs heavily on the mind of a student; a patient facing major surgery in five days is unable to relax and enjoy himself.

When one's future is dark, the present is likewise darkened. This is clear if you think of the mental state of airplane passengers who learn their aircraft is doomed. No meal could taste good to them, and no movie, however hilarious, could entertain. What might otherwise have been a pleasant trip has been transformed completely. Fearful and anxious, the passengers are thrown into confusion, some of them shrieking in terror. In this case the root of their suffering is the impending crash, but fiery death is not the only horror: the flight toward tragedy is itself a kind of hell.

To repeat, when the future is dark, the present is likewise darkened. The darkness of the present is owing to the darkness of the future. Anxiety about what may lie beyond death is inseparable from anxiety in the here and now. It stands to reason, therefore, that efforts to make the present bright without resolving this darkness of mind can only come to nothing.

When he was nearly fifty, the great Russian writer Leo Tolstoy (1828–1910) came to this very realization. Knowing that death might strike today or tomorrow, how could anyone rest easy? Shocked at this discovery, he lost all interest in work.

> I simply felt astonished that I had failed to realize this from the beginning. It had all been common knowledge for such a long time. Today or tomorrow sickness and death will come (and they had already arrived) to those dear to me, and to myself, and nothing will remain other than the stench and the worms. Sooner or later my deeds, whatever they may have been, will be forgotten and will no longer exist. What is all the fuss about then? How can a person carry on living and fail to perceive this? That is what is so astonishing! It is only possible to go on living while you are intoxicated with life; once sober it is impossible not to see that it is all a mere trick, and a stupid trick![74]

Sooner or later, even my precious family must come up against death: that thought took away Tolstoy's joy in his family and in his art, the two things that had previously sustained him. His writing had been going well, but once he took a long, hard look at the inevitability of death, his world shattered into a thousand pieces.

Pascal expressed his misgivings this way: "We run carelessly to the precipice, after we have put something before us to prevent us seeing it."[75] Indeed, we are like runners going full tilt in pitch-darkness. Without masking our cold fear of the unknown—the answer to the question "What will become of me after death?"—we cannot go on living. The advances of material civilization may make life easier, but they certainly cannot provide lasting happiness; they may mask the darkness temporarily, but they do not eliminate it. They are simply different ways of masking our fear. No such distraction is permanent, in fact, nor does it solve anything. Whatever we may turn our hand to lasts only for a flash, and we can find no heart's ease, living in a fleeting world that is like a burning house.

THE CRUCIAL MATTER OF THE AFTERLIFE

If a man's birth could be likened to an airplane lifting off from an aircraft carrier, then a lifetime of fighting desperately against heavy odds would correspond to a struggle against air turbulence and tempests, amid skirmishes with enemy planes. After a fierce fight, the pilot returns, only to find the carrier gone without a trace. Nothing meets his eye but the vast ocean. His fuel gauge reads zero. He looks back on the long, desperate struggle he has just endured, wondering what it was for, and curses himself for a fool.

"As life ends, regret and fear occur by turns." These words from the Larger Sutra of Infinite Life surely sum up the frame of mind of the pilot as his plane crashes into the sea. Just as for an airplane there is no worse fate than a crash, so in life there is no event of greater consequence than death. That is why Buddhism speaks of the "crucial matter of birth-and-death," or the "crucial matter of the afterlife."

We have squandered our days. We have sought the wrong objectives. Talent, property, and power have earned us the respect of others without affording us either joy or satisfaction. Why have we not rather sought happiness to satisfy the soul? We are left with nothing but sighs of regret. So wrote Seneca, a Roman philosopher who lived in the first century.[76] This lament can only be the regret of someone taken aback by the blackness of his prospects after death (darkness of mind).

This is the pitfall that no one sees coming until the last curtain of life. Perhaps that is what prompted Russian writer Anton Chekhov (1860–1904) to write, "Life is a vexatious trap."[77]

In the Larger Sutra of Infinite Life we also read, "People of this world are shallow and vulgar, struggling over things of no urgency." In other words, completely distracted by what is in front of their noses, people do not realize the essential task of life: to eliminate darkness of mind. This is the alarm sounded by Śākyamuni Buddha.

Shinran declared authoritatively that the root of suffering is darkness of mind, and that to eliminate this darkness and gain lasting happiness is the purpose of human life. The truth of this teaching should now be apparent.

Once we know this crucial matter of birth-and-death, debates over whether or not life has a purpose are beside the point. For indeed, at that very moment the purpose of life will be thrust upon us with unmistakable clarity.

CHAPTER 7

The Tragedy at Rājagṛha and the Vow of Amida

> Amida's inconceivable Vow is a great ship that carries us across the sea that is difficult to cross.[78]

With this declaration, Shinran opens his monumental work *Teaching, Practice, Faith, Enlightenment*. It means that Amida's Vow to save all beings, which eradicates darkness of mind, is a great ship in which all are borne cheerfully and happily across life's sea of endless waves of tribulation. The purpose of living is precisely to board this ship.

Shinran then comments on the story of the tragedy at Rājagṛha that took place more than twenty-five hundred years ago during the lifetime of Śākyamuni, the historical Buddha. As we will see, the heroine of that story, Queen Vaidehī, is finally lifted onto the ship, thus attaining the purpose of her life.

* * *

Long ago the ancient kingdom of Magadha, ruled by King Bimbisāra (543–491 BC), was supreme in the subcontinent of India. Bimbisāra was a mighty ruler whose influence extended in all directions, and Vaidehī, his consort, was as lovely as a flower. The pair lived together in the palace in the capital of Rājagṛha, lacking for nothing, seemingly as happy as any two people could be. Yet they shared one great sorrow which they endured in silence: for years, no child was born to them.

Childlessness is a common enough affliction, but for a royal couple it is a calamity. What could be more devastating than to think that on one's death, power would be wrested away from one's ancestral line, with perhaps fearful consequences? For King Bimbisāra and Queen Vaidehī, whose kingdom held sway over all others, each passing year brought greater anxiety as their thoughts turned helplessly to the future. Finally, not knowing what else to do, they sought the aid of a fortune-teller. As so often happens, anxiety over the future led them astray.

In response to the couple's earnest pleas, the fortune-teller pondered a while and then told them, "Do not worry. A child will be born to you." The king and queen leaned forward with excitement, hardly daring to believe it was true. The soothsayer went on, "There is now an aged ascetic living deep in the mountains. The child will be born as soon as his life runs out."

"How soon is that?" they asked eagerly.

"Another five years."

At that, their smiles faded. The queen's disappointment was especially keen, for she was nearing an age when motherhood would no longer be possible. There could be no more waiting. She must have her child now. Her patience stretched to the limit, she pleaded, "I cannot bear so long a wait! Can it not be sooner?"

Overpowered by her intensity, the fortune-teller blurted out, "There *is* one way …"

"Tell us. What must we do?" Now King Bimbisāra spoke, leaning forward intently.

"If the ascetic but dies sooner, your son's birth will be hastened by that much. But I could never recommend such a course of action. Listen to me!" With desperate insistence, the fortune-teller denied having been the one to bring up the idea.

"If the ascetic but dies sooner …" The king murmured the words over to himself. After mulling it over, the next day he gathered his council to seek their advice.

One man spoke up: "We too are eager for the appearance of an heir, but surely to kill an ascetic for that purpose would be going too far. Why not be patient a while longer?"

The majority likewise cautioned against a rush to violence. King Bimbisāra listened thoughtfully to this counsel, apparently swayed by it, until Queen Vaidehī came up, tugged hard on his sleeve, and led him off into an adjoining room. "Pull yourself together!" she snapped, fuming.

"Why so angry, my dear?"

"Are you blind? Do you not see what is going on?" The queen had worked herself into a rage.

The king blinked in surprise.

"You cannot tell that you are being deceived!"

"What talk is this?"

"Think—in five years I will be too old for childbearing."

King Bimbisāra, having never considered this point, was instantly contrite. Pressing her advantage, the queen triumphantly added: "Those men are plotting to take over the throne. Have you not figured it out?"

The king sensed now the direction his wife's thoughts were taking, but still he attempted to placate her. "That may be true, my dear, but still—to murder another human being—and a holy man at that!"

His words only stoked the flames of her ambition and increased her fierce longing for a child. "Don't be silly," she said. "Just think of the many wars you have fought over small patches of land, and the number of lives lost then! This is a far worthier cause—a successor for you! Why, the whole nation will rejoice."

Hearing his wife bring up the past made the king uncomfortable. As he squirmed, she let slip something else: "I know it seems cruel toward the holy man, but after all, what real pleasure in life could there be for someone so old? How much greater his joy, surely, to be reborn as our child! Death will come as a blessing."

A self-centered view if ever there was one—but as history shows, power often blinds people to all but their own logic. Then disobedience, or failure to please, results all too often in summary execution. Queen Vaidehī provides an object lesson in the arrogance, brutality, and malice of the powerful. And so, like one who is a bodhisattva on the outside and a demon within, this gentle queen, who had never harmed a fly, readily conceived a plan steeped in horror. One is reminded of the haiku:

With voice so pure
does it yet devour lizards?
Spring cuckoo[79]

At his wife's urging, King Bimbisāra made up his mind to carry out the murder, and together they set off for the mountains with a unit of soldiers behind. They found the old ascetic meditating atop a rock, and drew near. King Bimbisāra called out to him in a patronizing tone, "Holy man! Very impressive!"

The old ascetic looked up in surprise at the sudden appearance of the king and queen, riding on a white elephant. He greeted them and inquired what brought their highnesses so deep into the mountains.

King Bimbisāra responded arrogantly, "I will tell you why we have come so far—for your own sake! You may not know it, but you are destined to be reborn as our son in the next life. The sooner the better, would you not say?"

Naturally, the ascetic turned down the offer straightaway. "No, thank you. Wherever I am to be born in the next life, I do not wish to die until I have completed the rigors of my training in this one."

Nobody, no matter how low in station, could be so foolish as to submit uncomplainingly to such an unreasonable command. But what ruler would be so lenient as to overlook out-and-out disobedience? In a fit of rage, King Bimbisāra spluttered, "No one who crosses me shall live!" He turned to his men and gave the order to kill.

The hapless ascetic was no more eager for death than you or I would be. Blood spurting from his body, he stared at the king and queen in horror and screamed a curse at them before dying, swearing revenge.

* * *

Soon thereafter, Queen Vaidehī conceived a child. Rejoicing filled the palace and the entire kingdom, as people everywhere looked forward gladly to the birth of an heir. Only the queen could not be happy—no, not even though her yearning for a child was finally to be satisfied. Besides the natural worries she felt over giving birth at a late age, she shuddered to think what fate she might suffer for having forced her husband to kill the old ascetic. Night and day, the sound of his dying curse rang in her ears. She sank deeper and deeper into depression, unable to eat or sleep. Often she would shake the sleeping king awake to pour out her woes, clinging fast to him:

"I am too terrified to sleep and I can hardly bear the sight of food. Could this be the doing of that ascetic? I am so frightened!"

King Bimbisāra did his best to console his trembling, distracted wife. "No use worrying over trifles, my dear. You will only harm your health. Believe me, everyone who is killed acts that way. Who would die with a thank-you on his lips? You are upset because you had never seen such a thing before, that is all …"

The days and months went by. Soon it was the month of her confinement, but Queen Vaidehī only felt a stronger agitation. Weeping, she implored her husband to consult the fortune-teller again. "Once more, that's all I ask. If only I knew more about the child I am carrying, I could relax."

Not knowing what else to do, the king complied with her request. The fortune-teller, quickly summoned, frowned and delivered himself of this prophecy: "The infant is definitely a prince, but inside the womb he is filled with resentment. When he is grown he will wreak harm upon you both."

The queen shuddered: her worst fear had been confirmed. To think that the child they had prayed for, longed for—committed murder for—was now to become a dreaded foe! Her own actions had brought the situation squarely on herself, but that never occurred to Queen Vaidehī. She only sought release from her fears. Her back to the wall, she again thought of a desperate measure, and forced her husband to agree.

"I cannot give birth to a son that will kill its parents," she announced. "How could we possibly rear him? The best thing to do is kill the child before any attachment forms. Make a delivery room on the upper floor, with a number of swords standing on the floor of the room beneath, so that as soon as the child leaves the womb it will fall on them and die. We have no other choice."

The king too had been tearing his hair out, wondering what to do. He felt pity for his unborn son, but in the end he agreed with his wife.

And so her time came, and she gave birth in the upper story room as planned.

As this story shows, when people feel cornered, there is no telling what they may do. The classic treatise *Lamenting the Deviations* contains this confession: "Under the right conditions, I, Shinran, would do anything."[80] In other words, given a compelling set of conditions, Shinran knew himself capable of any deed, however horrible. It is a truth that surely applies to all who have ever lived.

The child must have been meant to be born into this world after all, for it only lost the little finger of its right hand on the swords. Its life was miraculously spared.

From the moment they heard their son's lusty birth cries, all thought of infanticide fled the royal couple's hearts. They became the most doting of parents, and named the baby Ajātaśatru. Naturally, strict silence was imposed to keep details of his conception and birth from leaking out.

* * *

Prince Ajātaśatru was born with a wicked streak of violence. He was forever lashing out at his parents and caretakers, and he slew vassals as if they were bugs. His mouth was filled with harsh language, lies, and slander. Day in and day out he gave himself over to lustful pleasures, and his inhumanity knew no bounds. He terrorized the retainers until gradually the reins of power fell into his hands.

In mortal fear of their brutal and ungrateful son, the king and queen foresaw a gloomy future for their country and themselves, and they longed for inner peace. As souls in darkness crave the light, King Bimbisāra and Queen Vaidehī finally began a quiet search for true happiness. Such searches are always rewarded, and so was theirs: they encountered Śākyamuni Buddha as he traveled preaching in the kingdom, and listened to his sermons. His teachings fell on their parched and dusty hearts like a gentle, soaking rain.

"Only he can give illumination to the heart."

Deeply stirred by the depth and breadth of his teachings, King Bimbisāra and Queen Vaidehī became lay followers of the Buddha, pious keepers of his precepts. With their conversion came a dramatic rise in the numbers of his listeners. But at the same time, enemies of the Buddha arose, for "the wind envies a tall tree."

One of the worst was Devadatta, a cousin of Śākyamuni (eldest son of Śuklodana-raja, younger brother of Śākyamuni's father Śuddhodana-raja). Ambitious by nature, Devadatta grew jealous of his cousin's power and fame. Finally he conceived the idea of killing the Buddha to install himself as his successor and take over leadership of the community of believers. His heart was a cauldron filled with flames of envy and rage—flames that lurk in every human heart. These flames are quick to spread in all directions, becoming an inferno that devours all in its path.

One day Devadatta tried to assassinate the Buddha by throwing rocks from a mountaintop as he passed below, but managed only to injure the holy man's little toe. Next he set loose a herd of drunken elephants, hoping his cousin would be trampled to death, but this scheme also failed. Trunks aloft, the maddened elephants ran amok, making the very earth thunder, but the moment they encountered the Buddha's beneficence they lowered their trunks docilely and knelt down without doing him any harm.

Despite having failed not once but twice to take the life of the Buddha, Devadatta was still not ready to give up. "Where lies the ultimate source of his power?" he asked himself. "It must be the conversion of the royal couple. In that case, the best way to bury him is to bring about their downfall. But they are the two most powerful people in all the land. What can I do?"

Suddenly he slapped his knee in delight, thinking of their son Ajātaśatru. What better way to accomplish his goal? Devadatta was privy to all the details of the prince's birth. He proceeded to worm his way into the confidences of the prince with the poise of a master actor. The young and inexperienced Ajātaśatru was putty in his hands.

One day when the two were alone, Devadatta asked the prince if he knew what had happened to the little finger of his right hand. Ever since he was old enough to wonder, the prince's questions about that missing finger had always met with evasion, and so his curiosity ran deep. He listened intently—thereby falling straight into the trap. Devadatta waxed eloquent, exaggerating the story and leading Ajātaśatru farther down the path of evil. "So you see," he summed up, "your parents murdered you in your previous life, and then they tried to kill you all over again in this life. What happened to that finger is certain proof."

His words hit home. Ajātaśatru was enraged, and ordered his father thrown into prison—with strict instructions that all food be withheld until he starved to death.

And so Bimbisāra, once all-powerful, suffered the ignominy of imprisonment. He had heard the Buddha preach lessons of impermanence, but this drastic overnight change in his own fortunes was greater than anything he had ever heard. Writhing in anguish, he felt the truth of Buddha's teaching in every fiber of his being. He pressed his palms together before the holy mountain outside his window where the Buddha was preaching, and prayed fervently for words of solace.

In response, Śākyamuni Buddha sent two of his disciples: Pūrṇa, foremost preacher of sermons, and Maudgalyāyana, foremost worker of wonders. Together the two men patiently explained to Bimbisāra the law of karma: "A seed never sown cannot grow. That which we reap is nothing but the fruit of our own actions." Finally made to see the evil of what he had done, Bimbisāra shed tears of bitter repentance.

Meanwhile, worried over her husband's dire situation, Vaidehī purified her skin and covered it with buckwheat flour, while slipping wine inside her accessories. Every day she used her status as royal consort to evade the eyes of the inspectors and convey nourishment to her husband in this way. Thanks to the secret ministrations of his wife and the disciples, King Bimbisāra was able to cling precariously to life, nourished in body and in spirit.

Three weeks went by. Suspecting nothing, Ajātaśatru checked one day to make sure that his father was dead, only to have the prison guard reveal what had been going on. Ajātaśatru let out a howl of rage. "Only a rebel protects a rebel—no matter if you are my mother!" He drew his sword and approached her menacingly.

He had fallen completely into Devadatta's trap.

His aides were appalled. The minister Candraprabha and the noted physician Jīvaka stood between Ajātaśatru and his mother, remonstrating with the prince. "One hears of men who murdered their fathers to take the throne," they said, "but what man would murder his own mother!" They warned him that if he committed such an outrage, they would have no choice but to take action of their own.

The prince reluctantly gave in, sheathing his sword, but his voice shook with fury as he issued a new command. "Very well then, her life is spared—but I want her thrown in the dungeon." With this, he left in a fury.

* * *

Confined in a dark chamber by her own child, Queen Vaidehī suffered severe mental distress. She flailed at the prison walls with her fists, torn by anger at her son, hatred for Devadatta, and worry over her husband; and she wept like one demented. Yet her convulsive sobs only echoed eerily off the walls.

Her face contorted in pain, she had no recourse but Śākyamuni Buddha. Desperately she prayed for deliverance, but all that came out of her mouth was a stream of complaints ending: "Śākyamuni, why do you still not come, when I am suffering so?" She seemed to feel that clearly he owed her that much, after all she had done for him.

"Today I will get to the heart of the matter." With these words, Śākyamuni launched into a sermon on the Lotus Sutra. The masses were listening raptly, hanging on his every word, when Queen Vaidehī's grievous cries struck his soul. With a penetrating flash he saw all that was in her heart, cut short his sermon, and went straight to Rājagṛha.

Why did he take this drastic action? Children playing on a cliff need rescuing less urgently than those who are drowning in churning floodwaters below. The Buddha's compassion reached out to and embraced Queen Vaidehī in the moment of her greatest desperation. By this action he also demonstrated the true purpose of his birth in this world—that is, the preaching of Amida's Vow.

One might suppose that Queen Vaidehī greeted the Buddha with tears of rapture, overwhelmed that he would have interrupted a sermon on the Lotus Sutra just for her—but instead, she started right in complaining: "I am the most wretched person on earth. After all I did to raise that boy, how could he abuse me this way, his own mother? What have I done? He is completely in the wrong. Why must I have such an ungrateful child?"

Śākyamuni listened wordlessly to her endless outpouring of grievances.

"He was always a good boy in his heart, though. It's that no-good Devadatta who put him up to this. *He* is the real villain. None of this would have happened if it were not for Devadatta!"

Then her resentment found a still more outlandish target. "Oh, Śākyamuni, how could you have someone like that for a cousin! It is because you are so eminent that he became envious in the first place and dreamed up this plot. That is why my husband and I have ended up like this." Having made all her charges, she dissolved in tears.

In sum, her argument went like this: "I am suffering now because of my child. My child did this terrible thing to me because of Devadatta. Devadatta came up with his monstrous plan because of you, Śākyamuni Buddha. My suffering is therefore all your fault!"

While asking for his help she was pelting him with stones of resentment, though she remained unaware of doing any such thing. As he listened to her sad and foolish ranting, Buddha only gazed at her with infinite compassion through half-closed eyes. This is what has been called the "Sermon Without Words." No one knew better than he that sometimes silence can communicate more effectively than the most eloquent speech.

People are continually being amazed at outcomes in their lives, while remaining utterly unaware of seeds they have planted in the past. The story of the tragedy at Rājagṛha brings out the depths of human foolishness, weakness, and selfishness.

Queen Vaidehī longed for a word from the Buddha—anything at all would bring her solace. She begged, but he remained silent. Was he even listening? Her words seemed like balls bouncing off a stone wall. In frustration and chagrin, she tumbled deeper into an abyss of sorrow.

Exhausted in body and soul, she flung herself at his feet in despair. "Why was I ever born? My life is hell on earth. Oh, may I never be born into such hell again! Please let me go to a world without suffering."

To this heartfelt plea Śākyamuni Buddha finally responded: from the mark of the Buddha between his eyebrows he sent forth a flood of light illuminating the lands of all the Buddhas in the ten directions of the universe. Queen Vaidehī gazed raptly at the scene and said with a sigh of admiration, "How wonderful they are!" Among them all, she was drawn to one that outshone the rest. That, Śākyamuni told her, was the Pure Land of Amida, who reigns supreme among all Buddhas. Eagerly she asked, "What must I do to be born there? Only tell me, and I will do it!"

To awaken in one and all the single desire to be born in the Pure Land of Amida was always Śākyamuni's purpose; now, hearing her say the very words he had been waiting for, he let a smile of satisfaction play about his lips for the first time. He then proceeded to tell her what we know as the Sutra of Contemplation on the Buddha of Infinite Life, about Amida and his Pure Land.

* * *

"Vaidehī, Amida is to be found not far from here. When your mind's eye is opened, you will see that he is always beside you. Concentrate with all your heart on Amida and his Pure Land. Through my teachings I will show how you, and all those yet to come, may achieve rebirth there."

He began by urging on her the practice of virtue. He spoke of two kinds of virtue, "virtue of the settled mind" and "virtue of the scattered mind." The former means to quiet one's deluded mind and concentrate on Amida and his Pure Land through seated meditation or visualization; there are thirteen ways of practicing it. The latter means to refrain from evil and pursue good with a still-unquiet mind. It is the endeavor to say or do good things such as refraining from eating meat or fish, telling no lies, and the like; there are three ways of practicing it.

Once she had glimpsed the Pure Land of Amida, Queen Vaidehī asked the Buddha to tell her what she must do to go there, confident— or conceited enough to think—that she could really do whatever he said. She had no conception of herself as someone who could do only evil, whose only possible destination was Hell. This supreme arrogance and ignorance concerning one's own true nature is another manifestation of darkness of mind. (For an explanation of this, see Chapter 19.) As we have seen, darkness of mind is the source of all suffering. Darkness of mind cannot be destroyed by any exercise of the intellect, the emotions, or the will.

Śākyamuni Buddha understood full well the vainglorious nature of the human heart. From the outset, he refrained from telling the queen straight out that she was capable only of evil, instead saying, "If you think you can do it, go ahead and try." He taught her to perform the thirteen kinds of virtue of the settled mind, knowing through and through that she could never carry them out. One by one he explained them, saying, "If you do this, your sins will disappear and you can enter the Pure Land of Amida. Now try."

Vaidehī made a valiant effort, but the more she tried to focus her thoughts, the more she found herself engulfed in anger and hatred for Ajātaśatru and Devadatta. Not a particle of good came of all her efforts—which was only to be expected. How could a woman like Vaidehī, the incarnation of greed, anger, and discontent, hope to produce good on her own?

Then why had Śākyamuni Buddha set her this impossible task? True salvation cannot be obtained by human effort, yet Vaidehī was vain enough to believe that she could indeed be saved through her own efforts. The only way to demonstrate to her the foolishness of this belief was to allow her to actually try. Buddha's dealings with the queen shine with irresistible compassion.

Vaidehī sincerely tried to follow Buddha's instructions, but she found it completely impossible. Once she saw herself as hopelessly evil, she fell into a bottomless despair. Seeing into her heart, the earthly Buddha rejoiced that the time had finally come to tell her of Amida's Vow, which is for those in precisely such agony as hers. Just before he began to preach the seventh visualization of the lotus seat, he instructed Vaidehī to listen carefully and said, "I shall now reveal to you the great truth that will put an end to your suffering." At that very moment, his figure vanished, and in its stead was the golden resplendence of Amida himself. The moment she beheld the form of Amida, Queen Vaidehī's darkness of mind was lifted; her mind filled with joy and she could do nothing but weep in gratitude at Amida's boundless saving compassion. "Ah, how great the wonder! That someone as evil as I am, with no hope of salvation, could be saved … It is all due to the wondrous power of Amida's Vow!"

The great truth of which Śākyamuni Buddha had spoken was Amida's Vow, which alone has power to destroy the darkness of mind that is the root of all suffering, and thus enable us to fulfill the purpose of human life.

In her joy, she breathed thanks even to Ajātaśatru and Devadatta, without whom she would never have become capable of listening to the Buddha: "Full of resentment, hatred and bitterness as I was, I knew nothing of my real self. There has never been anyone as evil as I."

As it is written, "He who sees the form of Buddha, gains the mind of Buddha." To see the sacred form of Amida Buddha is to gain his mind of infinite compassion.

The Buddha's teachings on the sixteen ways of visualization (virtue of the settled mind and virtue of the scattered mind) contained in the Sutra of Contemplation on the Buddha of Infinite Life represented his supreme method of instruction to prepare Queen Vaidehī to encounter the wonder of Amida's salvation. Once she had been given passage on the great ship of that vow across the sea of life's difficulties, and thus fulfilled the purpose of her life, the darkness of her resentment and bitterness turned instantly to the brightness of penitence and gratitude; she was reborn. What's more, her son was so amazed at the extent of his mother's transformation that he repented of his terrible misdeeds and experienced a profound conversion.

Shinran's declaration is clear: "Anyone can, no less than Queen Vaidehī, attain the three blessings [of joy, enlightenment, and faith]."[81] Through the miraculous saving power of Amida's Vow, *anyone at all* can achieve absolute happiness, just as Queen Vaidehī did.

CHAPTER **8**

Shinran's Fulfillment of Life's Purpose

After commenting on the tragedy at Rājagṛha, Shinran turns to his own experience, expressing his thankfulness at having encountered salvation in this heartfelt and vivid cry of joy:

> Ah, how hard it is, even in many lifetimes, to encounter the strong power of Amida's Vow! How hard it is, even in myriad aeons, to obtain faith that is true and real! Anyone blessed with this faith cannot help but rejoice at the benevolent workings [of Amida] since the distant past that have brought it into being.
>
> Had I remained covered by the net of doubt in this life as well, I should have had to keep wandering, lost, through vast aeons. How genuine, the true words of Amida that embrace us and never forsake us, the absolute doctrine that is surpassingly wonderful! Listen and believe without hesitation or delay.[82]

To paraphrase: "Ah … how wonderful! The life of joy that I, Shinran, sought for so long, through many lives and aeons, is now mine! This is absolutely due to Amida's great saving power that embraces all. I am overwhelmed with deepest gratitude. If this life too had ended without my dark mind clearing, for endless ages to come I should have gone on suffering. I must hurry to tell everyone this truth, let them know that this vast, shoreless world of the mind exists!"

The exclamation "Ah!" conveys inexpressible surprise and delight, the likes of which Shinran has never known before. The "strong power of Amida's Vow" refers to the vow made by Amida out of his intense desire to eliminate the root of suffering of all people, that they may achieve the purpose of life. "Faith that is true and real" refers to the life of joy that is obtained once the root of suffering is eliminated and life's purpose achieved, in accordance with Amida's Vow. Shinran understands this is no easy happiness, to be had after a mere century or two of searching; he understands that he has found what cannot be found "even in many life-times," gained what is hard to gain "even in myriad aeons." Having found and gained something so impossibly rare and precious, it is only natural that he cannot repress a shout of sheer joy: "Ah!"

Then, thinking with emotion of how far back in the past Amida's grace extends, he can barely keep back tears of happiness: "Anyone blessed with this faith cannot help but rejoice at the benevolent workings [of Amida] since the distant past that have brought it into being."

There is a saying that the higher the mountain, the deeper the valley. From the great height of the mountaintop of his salvation, Shinran feels a thrill of amazement at the depth of the valley of darkness of mind. This is why he sighs, "Had I remained covered by the net of doubt in this life as well, I should have had to keep wandering, lost, through vast aeons." Here "net of doubt" is another way of saying "darkness of mind," the source of all suffering. Shinran marvels that if he had died without having his darkness of mind eliminated in this life by the power of Amida, he would surely have had to continue suffering for ages on end. It has truly been a narrow escape.

Reading these words, it is easy to picture Shinran with eyes shut and hands pressed together in fervent thanksgiving to Amida. He then de-clares, "How genuine, the true words of Amida that embrace us and never forsake us, the absolute doctrine that is surpassingly wonderful! Listen and believe without hesitation or delay." This means, "It is real! It is true! Amida's Vow is not a lie. Everyone must hear—I, Shinran, am a living witness. I want everyone to quickly know the truth of Amida's Vow."

Shinran has gone beyond fulfilling the purpose of his life. This beautiful confession overflows with his deep excitement at fulfilling, through the power of Amida, not just the purpose of this life but that of "many lives and myriad aeons."

THE VAST OCEAN OF DAZZLING BRIGHTNESS

Shinran also uses the analogy of ocean and ship in praise of Amida's Vow:

> Now that I have boarded the ship of Amida's great
>   compassion,
> now that I am afloat on the vast ocean of brightness,
> the breezes of supreme joy blow softly
> and the waves of all woe are transformed.[83]

"Lifted aboard the ship of Amida's great pity, I look on the sea of suffering that is my life and see a vast ocean of dazzling brightness. How wonderful it is to be alive, like voyaging over the sea with a fair wind in the sails!" This is Shinran's log of a radiantly happy journey by sea.

"Now that I have boarded the ship of Amida's great compassion" is a glad declaration that he has fulfilled the purpose of life in accordance with Amida's Vow. Clearly, the purpose of life is by no means vague. "Now that I am afloat on the vast ocean of brightness" expresses his joy in having his dark life changed to one of bright rejoicing. Only one who has wept at the darkness can laugh at encountering light; only one who has been buried in the depths of the sea can know the joy of floating on the surface of the water.

Why endure the sufferings of this life? Why go on living? This crucial thing eludes our understanding. Yet if we live only for the sake of living, what differentiates us from animals headed for the slaughterhouse? If we live only to await death, we are in fact buried beneath the waves.

What was the nature of the life experienced by Shinran once he had been borne to the surface of the "vast ocean of brightness" and freed from the agony of uncertainty over the meaning of life, rejoicing that he was born? His answer is brief and brimming with confidence: "The breezes of supreme joy blow softly and the waves of all woe are transformed." This is a paean to Amida for his gifts of radiant joy and vigor to overcome any difficulty in life.

Elsewhere, Shinran described the world of "soft breezes of supreme joy" thus:

> If anyone in this evil, corrupt world
> has faith in the Vow of Amida,
> unnamable, inexplicable, inconceivable
> blessing fills his being.[84]

In other words, "I, Shinran, am ridden with evil, yet with my dark mind now eradicated, joy beyond description swells continually within me."

Shinran is in ecstasy at having been saved by Amida's Vow. His absolute happiness causes him to place his palms together in endless thanksgiving. This day is blessed. Still more marvelous is his very breathing at this moment, each successive inhalation and exhalation a thing of wonder. The more clearly he sees his lack of a joyful mind, the more deeply he rejoices in his salvation. This paradox moves him deeply. He knows for a certainty that the purpose of life is entrance into this absolute state. This is the state of "twofold revelation," about which we will have more to say below (see Chapter 11).

The bliss bestowed by Amida that always fills him, and that can never be destroyed by fire, washed away by a tsunami, or stolen by a thief, he describes here in ringing words: "Unnamable, inexplicable, inconceivable blessing fills [Shinran's] being."

Finally, what does it mean that the "waves of all woe are transformed"? The nine decades of Shinran's life were full of vicissitudes. He was the object of constant derision, abusive taunts, oppression, and persecution. Even while coming under concentrated fire, he could only join his hands in gratitude to the marvelous power of Amida's Vow, which worked this perfect joy:

> Mindful solely of the depth of Amida's benevolence, I pay no
> mind to others' derision.[85]

"While receiving the immeasurable grace of Amida, I cannot return even the smallest particle of what was bestowed on me. Am I a monster of ingratitude, the scum of the earth? I must do something!"

Not even the fiercest billows in the sea of suffering could stop Shinran's progress as, moved to tears by the profound benevolence of Amida, he surmounted all difficulties with penitence and joy. Nor is that all: the turbulent waves causing him such distress were transformed into a source of happiness. (For further explanation of this point, see Chapter 23.)

THERE IS A GREAT SHIP

Surrounded only by sky and water, each of us is swimming for dear life in the sea, searching for a nearby log, stick, or board to cling to for support. All around are vast numbers of people similarly tormented by wind and waves, betrayed by the logs and sticks they have found, choking on saltwater, drowning or drowned. Offering earnest pointers to all who are floundering is an assortment of "swimming coaches": endeavors such as politics, economics, science, medicine, the arts, literature, and the law.

When will people be amazed at the absurdity that no one is asking the most important question: "What should we swim toward?" That is, "Why must we live?" The silence on this topic is life's greatest mystery, and surely humanity's greatest tragedy.

> The painful sea of birth-and-death knows no bounds.
> We have long been submerged.
> Only the ship of Amida's Vow
> will take us aboard and carry us across without fail.[86]

To paraphrase: "We have long been floundering, lost in the vastness of the ocean of suffering; the only thing that can take us aboard unconditionally and carry us to the far shore without fail is the Vow of Amida."

The Vow-ship sails across wave after towering wave; however high the waves, the ship is higher still. Shinran pointed out the real existence of this great ship that can rescue us, and the direction in which it lies.

CHAPTER 9

Shinran's Masterwork Begins and Ends with a Cry of Joy

THE PURPOSE OF MYRIAD LIFETIMES

Buddhism teaches that from ages past, each of us has been born and reborn countless times in a myriad of life forms. Trapped in the cycle of birth and death, we have never known true happiness, which comes only from salvation through Amida's Vow. When salvation finally comes, we understand with joy how great a thing it is to be born human, since otherwise we should never have been able to achieve this lasting happiness. We see that truly, human life is infinitely "heavier than the heaviness of all things."

Indeed, the ultimate purpose of life has reference not just to this lifetime but to the eternal span of all our lifetimes, past, present, and future. These myriad lives, encompassing untold aeons, have all been for the sake of fulfilling a single purpose: to be delivered into absolute happiness through Amida's Vow. This overarching purpose can be realized only during human life, which is what makes this lifetime infinitely precious. The joy that pervades Shinran's writings stems from his awareness that the purpose of all his lifetimes from ages past has been gloriously fulfilled.

Such joy is permanent. All other pleasures fade.

Indeed, *Teaching, Practice, Faith, Enlightenment* begins and ends with a cry of pure joy: "How joyful I am!" One critic has written that "a voice of ecstasy permeates all volumes" of the work.[87] Here is the joyous voice of Shinran, "dancing on heaven and on earth."

How joyful I am, Gutokushaku[88] Shinran! Rare it is to encounter the scriptures from the westward land of India, and the commentaries of the masters in China and Japan, but now I have encountered them. Rare it is to hear them, but I have already been able to hear. Most of all, honoring and believing in the teaching, practice, and enlightenment[89] of the true religion, I have known the depths of Amida's grace. This being so, I can only rejoice in all I have heard, and exclaim in wonder at all I have gained.[90]

To paraphrase: Ah, how happy am I, Shinran! By Amida's power alone, I have now encountered what there was not the slightest chance of encountering. I have now heard what never could have been heard. However great the Vow of Amida that Śākyamuni preached, if there had been no one to convey it to me, the darkness of mind afflicting me would never have been dispelled. Buddhism is preached far and wide, but those who expound the true wonder of Amida's Vow are few and far between. Now I have been able to encounter the teachings of those rare priests in India, China, and Japan who expounded the wonder of Amida's Vow; I have been able to know the wonder of the Vow. To what can I compare this happiness? No amount of rejoicing would be too great. My heart is filled with Amida's deep benevolence. Somehow I must convey the wonder of Amida's Vow.

With these words Shinran recorded the state of mind that compelled him to write *Teaching, Practice, Faith, Enlightenment*, and then he proceeded to set down the six volumes of his masterwork.

THE INDESTRUCTIBLE GROUND OF THE VOW

After pouring his soul into each word of *Teaching, Practice, Faith, Enlightenment*, Shinran wrote the following postscript:

How joyful I am! My mind stands firm in the ground of Amida's Vow, and my thoughts flow through the unfathomable ocean of his Law. The more deeply I come to know of Amida's immense compassion, the greater my gratitude to the teachers who led me. My joy grows ever fuller, my debt weighs ever heavier …

Mindful solely of the depth of Amida's benevolence, I pay no mind to others' derision.

May those who encounter this book make their belief and obedience the cause, or their skepticism and revilement the condition, of attaining true faith through the power of the Vow and gaining the wonderful fruit of enlightenment in the Pure Land.[91]

Anyone who places his trust in unreliable things will suffer for it, as the following comic story illustrates.

Long ago, in the Chinese kingdom of Chu, a foolish fellow secretly brought out a sword that was a family treasure, took it on board a boat in a swift-flowing river, and commenced to try it out. He swung the sword so vigorously that it flew out of his hand and landed in the water with a splash. The current bore the boat speedily on. Taken aback, the man lost no time in whipping out his dagger and marking a deep notch on the gunwale where the sword had fallen overboard, muttering, "There! Now I can tell exactly where it is."

The point of the story is the foolishness of the man, who had no notion that the mark he made was itself in constant motion.

One who places trust in money and possessions is severely shaken when money and possessions are lost. One who places trust in honor and position suffers a terrible setback when those are lost. One who places trust in parents or children will collapse in despair when these are lost. One who places trust in convictions will suffer a breakdown when his convictions waver.

Shinran's postscript may be paraphrased as follows: The life built on things that will come to nothing is as precarious as a walk across thin ice. But how happy am I, Shinran! Even if the teachings of Śākyamuni, Shan-tao,[92] and Honen should prove false, I, with my mind set fast in the indestructible ground of the Vow, am assuredly alive in a wondrous world. The more I am shown of the depths of Amida's compassionate love, the deeper the gratitude I feel toward the teachers to whom I owe so much. My boundless joy brings me to tears at the

thought of the debt I can never repay. In the face of Amida's great beneficence, the slights and derision of others count for nothing. Readers of
this book will surely include believers and skeptics alike. Either way, may
their state of mind prove cause or condition for them to encounter the
salvation of Amida and come into everlasting happiness. This is my constant desire.

With these words, *Teaching, Practice, Faith, Enlightenment* ends.

"Now I have encountered what is hard to encounter."
"Already I have heard what is hard to hear."
"I exclaim in wonder at all I have gained."
"My joy grows ever fuller, my debt weighs ever heavier."
Such statements of assurance from Shinran are worlds removed from
the vagueness of "I think" or "I am of the opinion that." The blazing
happiness that fills him tip to toe fairly leaps off the page. That is the
same reason for the fresh urgency of these lines:

> The grace of Amida's great compassion
> I must repay, though I grind my body to dust,
> and the grace of the teachers who led me
> I must also repay, though I crush my bones to bits.[93]

"The benevolence of Amida Buddha and those who have taught me
about his Vow can never be fully repaid, even if I were to grind my body
to dust and smash my bones to bits. Day and night I am brought to tears
at my own laziness, for not making a particle of recompense."

Shinran can only have met with Amida's salvation that eradicates the
dark mind—the root of all suffering—and fulfills the purpose of many
lives and myriad aeons. Nothing else could account for the deep ecstasy
and penitence, and the strong desire to repay an unpayable debt, that inform these words.

CHAPTER **10**

The Clash over Whether or Not Life Has a Purpose

THE PATH WITH NO END

"What? You mean that life has a distinct purpose? That there can be completion?" Most people are surprised to hear that life has a purpose that can be accomplished. This surprise is only natural, because common sense tells us just the opposite. If you think about it, any pursuit— whether learning or the arts, science or medicine, chess or *go*, fencing or judo, cooking or body-building—consists of an endless path, without possibility of final graduation or completion, whatever heights one may reach along the way. As the word itself implies, all our "pursuits" are lifelong paths with no end.

In 1998, the rock group B'z had the number one and two CD albums in Japan. Two years later, total sales of all their works topped seventy million—the equivalent of the fifth-best mark in U.S. recording history. Yet vocalist Koshi Inaba is not satisfied. In an interview to mark the debut of their album "Survive," he had this to say: "I always focus really hard on an album or a tour, and at the time I'll think, 'This is the greatest!' But when it's over, somehow I'm always like, 'Nope, still got a long way to go.'" Japanese ukiyoe painter Katsushika Hokusai (1760– 1849) lamented, looking back over his career, "If Heaven had only granted me five more years, I could have become a real painter."[94] And the French painter Renoir is reported to have said, on his deathbed, "I am still progressing."

Music and art are certainly not the only fields where there is no finishing point; pursuits such as learning and sports also have no final, consummating goal. This suits most people just fine. To think you had arrived at completion would be harmful, the argument goes, because it would mark an end to progress. The path with no end is the path most worth taking.

Let us examine that last proposition. In fact, to claim that "the path with no end is the path most worth taking" is to glorify the lifelong search for something that is one hundred percent unattainable. When you think about it, the idea is patently absurd. Any search must be predicated on the assumption that what is sought can be found. Anyone who would devote his entire life to the search for something he knew was unattainable might just as well keep on buying tickets to last year's lottery.

Some will insist that a search with no end suits them fine, because the process of lifelong betterment and striving is wonderful in itself. And yet such fulfillment is temporary and fugitive. It is different by nature from the joy in life that shouts out, "How glad I am I was born a human being!" Those who praise endless seeking do not know the joy of attaining life's true purpose.

LIFE WITHOUT REGRETS

Shinran once instigated a great debate over whether life does or does not have a purpose. Kakunyo (1270–1351; Shinran's great-grandson) wrote about it in *Notes on Oral Transmissions*, in a section opening with these words:

> The question of whether Amida's salvation occurs with or without loss of the body. Shinran said that when he was a disciple of the master Honen, a great dispute arose over this point of doctrine.[95]

When Shinran was one of Honen's disciples, he clashed with fellow disciple Zen'ebo over the purpose of life. Shinran declared unequivocally that this life has a purpose; Zen'ebo was adamant that it does not. Where Shinran asserted that "the purpose of life is to be saved through

Amida's Vow and achieve complete fulfillment," Zen'ebo asserted that "to be saved through Amida's Vow and achieve complete fulfillment in this life is impossible." Their conflict was thus inevitable.

It is known today as the "debate on whether Amida's salvation takes place with or without loss of the body."

Zen'ebo declared that Amida's salvation was unattainable in this life, and so his position is known as "salvation with loss of the body," that is, salvation after death. Shinran insisted that the purpose of life was indeed to be saved by Amida here and now, and so his position is called "salvation without loss of the body," that is, salvation during this lifetime.

The two men debated the issue hotly, Shinran maintaining that life does have a purpose (Amida's salvation), and Zen'ebo insisting otherwise. Their fellow disciples looked on in dire confusion and agitation. Did Amida's salvation occur in this lifetime or not? In other words, did human life itself have a purpose, or did it not? The question was so momentous that they had to go to their teacher Honen and settle it once and for all.

After listening to all the arguments on both sides, Honen made the following pronouncement: "To say there is no salvation until after death runs counter to the Vow of Amida. Amida vowed to grant the salvation of complete fulfillment in this life, and so human life does indeed have a most important purpose. Look at the text of the sutras, and you will see it stated clearly." Thus ended this great dispute over Buddhist doctrine, one of three that Shinran would instigate.

The reason Zen'ebo stated mistakenly that Amida's salvation could not possibly occur in this life was none other than this: he himself had never known the great joy of having his dark mind dispelled, or the complete fulfillment of entering into Amida's salvation. Therefore, he could only conceive of Amida's salvation on the same level with human interests, pursuits, and temporal goals. No wonder he pitted himself against Shinran, maintaining that Amida's salvation could never be completed during this lifetime.

Shinran, however, having already clearly fulfilled the purpose of life, could not let Zen'ebo's contention pass unchallenged. He was thinking not only of the influence of this eminent disciple, but of Zen'ebo's own welfare.

If there is no purpose in life—no salvation by Amida in this lifetime—then people are born only to suffer.

Life expectancy has greatly increased, but longer life is no guarantee of happiness. Some people work hard all their lives so that they can afford to eat fine food in retirement, only to contract diabetes and be forced to go on a restricted diet. Others plan and save for travel and a fancy wardrobe, only to end up paralyzed on one side of the body, confined to bed. Still others go into the hospital and have their children gather around, only to realize that their children's main concern is getting hold of their bankbook and money. Such people die with tears of regret, wondering what their life was all about.

> In the space between breaths is the next world. Once your life as a human is over, it will not return for ten thousand aeons. If you do not find enlightenment at this moment, how can the Buddhas save you? Let everyone think deeply on the mutability of life, and leave no vain regrets.[96]

To paraphrase: If your next breath fails to follow this one, you will be in the next life. Your human existence will have ended, never to return. Śākyamuni said, "Human form is hard to receive, Buddhist truth is hard to hear." Only human beings can encounter Amida's salvation. If you do not achieve the purpose of life now, when will you? When can you? Now is your only chance, for untold ages to come. Gaze steadily at the shadow of impermanence drawing closer every moment, and have no regrets.

The "debate on whether Amida's salvation occurs with or without loss of the body" can be summed up as a duel between Shinran's fellow disciple, who said this life has no purpose, and Shinran, who declared unequivocally that it does.

CHAPTER **11**

The Key to the Mystery of Why We Live

THE MIND WHERE NO MORE DARKNESS DWELLS

To describe the world of salvation, in which darkness of mind is dispelled and the purpose of life achieved, Shinran used the Buddhist term *ichinen*; the characters *ichi* and *nen* may be rendered separately as "one" and "heart." Darkness of mind he called *futagokoro*, or "double heart." In *Teaching, Practice, Faith, Enlightenment*, Shinran wrote, "*Ichinen* is so called because it does not have a double heart [*futagokoro*]."[97] *Ichinen* thus refers to the mind where no more darkness dwells.

When the darkness is gone, all is light. What once lay hidden is now open to view. When darkness of mind is dispelled, what comes to light? Two things: one's true self, and the truth of the Vow of Amida. In Buddhism this is called *nishu jinshin*, or "twofold revelation."

Thus the salvation of Amida expounded by Shinran consists of clear, unmistakable revelation of both one's true self and the truth of Amida's Vow. This point is crucial to understanding Shinran's faith, and so let us turn to his own words.

REVELATION OF THE TRUE SELF

I am, now, a foolish being imbued with evil and caught in the cycle of birth and death, constantly submerged and constantly wandering for all these countless aeons without ever a chance for liberation: this is clearly revealed to me.[98]

To paraphrase: I have come to see myself clearly as the vilest and most depraved of sinners, with absolutely no possibility of salvation in the past, present, or future. (For further explanation see below, beginning with Chapter 14.)

REVELATION OF THE TRUTH OF AMIDA'S VOW

> Amida Buddha's Forty-eight Vows embrace all beings, and so if I but ride on the power of the Vow without any doubt or apprehension I will attain birth in the Pure Land: this is clearly revealed to me.[99]

To paraphrase: I have come to see clearly the reality of Amida's Vow to effect salvation into absolute happiness in this world and beyond. (For further explanation see below, beginning with Chapter 20.)

BELIEF VERSUS KNOWLEDGE

Jinshin, the word rendered here as "revelation," is written with characters meaning "deep" and "belief," and yet it does not mean "deep belief." There is a difference between belief and the sure knowledge that comes from revelation. We "believe" because we doubt. When there is no possibility of doubt, we say instead that we "know" something. A person covered with terrible burns is unlikely to say, "I believe fire is hot." He knows very well from experience that it is so. A principal who says, "I believe there is no bullying in my school," puts it that way because he suspects that there may in fact be bullying. Revelation is different. It means the receiving of knowledge beyond all shadow of doubt. That is why Shinran wrote, "I know in truth," and Rennyo, "Now I clearly know." Such knowledge has nothing whatever to do with efforts to swallow one's doubts and force oneself to believe.

Shinran's writings are permeated with passages extolling twofold revelation—that is, the simultaneous revelation of one's true self and of the truth of Amida's Vow. Without an understanding of twofold revelation, *Teaching, Practice, Faith, Enlightenment* and all his other writings would be unintelligible. One might read them but wind up with a distorted idea of his message. Because twofold revelation is so important, we will examine it closely in the following chapters.

CHAPTER 12

Turning a Blind Eye to Ourselves

WHAT WE OUGHT TO BUT DO NOT KNOW

Once a person's dark mind clears, two things become apparent. One of these, according to Shinran, is the truth about oneself.

Who or what is the "real me"? What could be more important than knowing this? The German philosopher Ernst Cassirer (1874–1945) began his *An Essay on Man* with this assertion: "That self-knowledge is the highest aim of philosophical inquiry appears to be generally acknowledged … This objective … [has] proved to be the Archimedean point, the fixed and immovable center, of all thought."[100]

"I know myself better than anyone else ever could," we assume. Yet the continuing relevance of the ancient Greek admonition to "know thyself" suggests strongly that in fact we humans understand ourselves very little, if at all. We may understand distant workings of the universe, we may elucidate the world of subatomic particles, we may determine sequences of the three billion chemical base pairs that constitute human DNA—and yet the one thing we still cannot pin down is the self.

Not long ago, Japanese TV screens were filled with the pitiful image of a live wild duck with an arrow embedded in its flesh, evidently the doing of a cruel prankster. Across the nation, viewers' hearts went out to the hapless creature. One day in a restaurant we saw someone stare at a TV image of the duck and grimace, saying, "How could anyone be so mean to an animal"—all the while helping himself to savory duck hotpot. The lesson that people truly do not see themselves was brought home with force. Such self-contradiction is everywhere.

The following conversation took place between an elderly husband and wife living in the countryside. Husband: "In the old days, the rooster always used to crow at sunrise, and tell us the time." Wife: "Yes, nowadays even roosters are lazy good-for-nothings. It's awful." Neither realized that the problem was their own growing deafness.

> Certain though we are
> that this one thing above all else
> is what we know the best,
> the one thing most unknowable
> is nothing but the self.

In all ages and all countries, stories have been told mocking the foolishness of those who do not know themselves, precisely because the condition is so universal. Here are some more examples.

Long ago in India, the scion of a wealthy family took a lovely wife. After their marriage, the newlyweds indulged in wine to add even more sensuality to the pleasures of the bed. One night, the bride went as usual to the wine-jar and removed the lid; she was about to ladle up more wine when lo and behold, there inside the wine-jar was a seductive young woman. Assuming her husband had been cheating on her, she began to berate him, weeping and shrieking and carrying on. The bemused husband took one look in the jar and saw the face of a lusty young man. Assuming his wife had taken a lover, he began casting loud aspersions on her chastity. In the heat of their quarrel, the jar tipped over and shattered, and that put an end to the matter. Each had been too inebriated to recognize his or her own face reflected in the wine.

Long ago in China, a minister was famous for his splendid beard. The emperor inquired one day whether he customarily slept at night with the beard tucked inside the covers or lying out on top, and the minister found himself unable to answer. To answer the question properly, he requested one night's grace, went straight home, and climbed into bed to experiment. When he tucked the beard under the covers he could hardly breathe, and with it lying on top of the covers he felt awkward. The beard was long and full; all night long he tucked it in and took it out again by turns, unable to make up his mind.

One day a gang of thieves was holding a banquet in their mountain hideout. Naturally the room was filled with stolen articles. Among the booty was a shining gold goblet. As the men passed it around, each taking a drink from it in turn, at some point the goblet disappeared. The leader jumped up with a ferocious scowl and yelled, "Somebody here is a crook!" He could hardly have said such a thing had he remembered his own position as leader of a gang of thieves.

It is hard not to identify with stories such as these. Kierkegaard warned that "the biggest danger, that of losing oneself, can pass off in the world as quietly as if it were nothing."[101] We forget to remove the cash from an ATM and make a great to-do about it, but forget what is most important, our own self, without the least concern.

IN THE PRESENCE OF THE SPHINX

Once as Śākyamuni Buddha was resting in the shade of a tree, a group of thirty or so noblemen and their wives were enjoying a drinking party in a nearby grove. One of the group, a bachelor, had brought with him a woman of loose morals who, when the drunken revelers fell asleep, seized the chance to make off with everyone's valuables. Shocked at the discovery of what had happened, the entire group set off, determined to track her down. When they came upon the Buddha, they asked him whether he had seen a suspicious woman go by. His response brought them quickly to their senses: "I understand the situation, but which is more important? Finding that woman, or finding yourself?" Their eyes were opened; they sat down and listened to the Buddha preach, and all became his disciples on the spot, according to scripture.

The Sphinx that maintains eternal silence in the sands of Egypt was, in Greek legend, a monster that devoured all travelers unable to answer this riddle: "What creature walks on four legs in the morning, two legs at noon, and three in the evening?" In other words, the Sphinx confronted human beings with the question, "What is a human being?" It is a question for which politics, economics, science, medicine, literature, philosophy, and religion have all sought to provide answers. Each person must answer it for himself or herself. In the presence of the Sphinx, no one may speak for another, and no parroting of others' words is allowed.

CHAPTER 13

The Difficulty of Knowing Oneself

SEEING OURSELVES THROUGH OTHERS' EYES

Why is it so hard to know oneself?

The human eye is designed to see a great many things, but anything too distant or too close is out of sight. As the saying goes, "The eye cannot see itself, nor the sword cut itself." Directly below the lighthouse beam that shines for a thousand leagues, all is dark. In the same way, we can see others with clarity but are utterly blind to ourselves. What lies closest at hand is invisible.

To get around the difficulty of seeing ourselves, we use mirrors. What sort of mirror comes to mind as a tool for us to know ourselves? Perhaps nothing has so powerful an effect on us as what other people say. How others view us is something we constantly fret and worry over. Parents everywhere want their children to grow up to be respectable members of society; in Japan, parents habitually caution their offspring against inviting ridicule. In fact, there is universal faith in the mirror of others' opinions as a means of self-knowledge.

But do others make a just evaluation? Can they? What writings from the Tokugawa era (1600–1867) portray benevolent aspects of the rule of powerful warlord Toyotomi Hideyoshi (1537–98)? What early Meiji (1868–1912) writings sing the praises of the Tokugawa shogunate? History is always written from the perspective of the victor.

A transfer of power means a corresponding change in values. In the Tokugawa period, *chu* ("loyalty") meant to die for one's shogun or feudal lord. From the late nineteenth century through the end of World War II, this same word meant to sacrifice one's life for the emperor, and was the standard for moral behavior. Anyone in Japan who touted the doctrine of popular sovereignty, or the equality of labor and management, would have been thrown in jail for holding "dangerous views"— and yet today, the emperor and the laborer are equal under Japanese law. When a regime changes, the constitution may change; prisoners may be released overnight in a general amnesty; yesterday's men of power may be today's condemned convicts.

The Zen monk Ikkyu wrote this verse mocking the way people's value judgments fluctuate:

> The human tongue
> gives praise today, tomorrow
> it finds fault—
> laugh away or weep away,
> it is all a tissue of lies.

We call someone "good" when it suits us, and when it does not, we brand the same person "bad." Do we not pass judgment on others to suit our own convenience? Our judgments alter in accord with our fluctuating heart. Thus it often happens that yesterday's ally is today's enemy.

German-American political philosopher Hannah Arendt (1906–75) is famous for her 1951 work on Nazism titled *The Origins of Totalitarianism*. She is also known for the illicit affair she had with philosopher Martin Heidegger (1889–1976), who was a married man with a family. Heidegger had been a member of the Nazi party, for which he was harshly condemned by Jews and others. Despite his egregious conduct towards the Jews, Arendt—herself a Jew—consistently defended him. As the saying goes, "Better a lie from the one I love than the truth from one I hate." Even an eminent scholar like Arendt apparently could not think that the actions of the man she loved were evil.

There is a constant danger of subjectivity in others' evaluations. Supreme Court decisions, made by veteran jurists, are seldom if ever unanimous. We like to think our courts dispense impartial justice, but even though the facts of a case remain the same, the verdict often flip-flops as the case wends its way through the appeals system. Obviously, the deciding factor is the subjective consciousness of the judges.

"A pig that is praised is still a pig; a lion scorned is a lion yet." This saying aptly derides the foolishness and irresponsibility of opportunistic, self-serving value judgments.

THE MIRROR OF THE CONSCIENCE

Once we accept that the mirror of others' evaluations is not fully trust-worthy, where else can we turn for a mirror in which to see our true selves? People have consciences, and it is possible to view humans as ani-mals capable of self-reflection using the mirror of conscience. But can the conscience function as a mirror that shows the unadorned self?

One day a princess in the legendary Dragon Palace under the sea held up a jewel and told all the fishes, "I will give a prize to anyone who can tell me what color this is." Each of them named a different color: the black porgy said it was black, the bluefish said it was blue, and the white-fish said it was silver. Then they asked the princess, "Which one is right?" She replied, "The jewel has no color of its own. It is transparent, and simply reflects each of your colors."

Similarly, we are unable to see anything except through the prism of thought and emotion. When it comes to examining ourselves in particu-lar, it is impossible to take off the tinted glasses of partiality and self-seeking. Egoism clouds our vision.

Examples abound. Here is a true story we heard recently from an ac-quaintance who is a physician. A high school girl came to the hospital in the middle of the night complaining of abdominal pain. It quickly be-came apparent to our acquaintance, the doctor on call, that she was go-ing into labor. When he told this to the girl's mother, she gave him a withering look and declared, "Not *my* daughter!" The girl admitted that it was true, however, sending her mother into shock as they headed off to the obstetrics department. The woman's vanity and self-righteousness had led her to dismiss her daughter's condition as mere "chubbiness," and kept her from judging the situation correctly.

Not *my* son! Not *my* daughter! This smug assumption forms the perfect breeding ground for juvenile crime. Assuming that it is impossible for anyone to view his or her own child objectively, many people shrug off such cases, saying, "Well, that's a parent for you." If people are unable to be impartial about their children, it may be inferred how lenient they are with themselves.

We all find things about ourselves to take pride in. I may have bad skin, we say, but at least my nose is nice. Or, I may have bad skin and a snub nose, but at least my mouth is nice. Or, I may have a big mouth, but at least I have dimples. In the end we may say, I'm not good for much of anything, but at least people say I am a "regular fellow." The first gray hairs we find in the mirror give us pause, but it is not long before we preen and think, "At least I haven't got as many as the woman next door!" At fifty we comfort ourselves by looking at someone who's sixty; at sixty, by looking at someone who's seventy, and at seventy, by looking at someone who's eighty—saying to ourselves, each time, "I look younger than *that*, anyway." Although words do not change a thing, we are charmed when anybody thinks we look younger than we are, and put off by anyone who guesses our age high.

A thief who prided himself on his agility, or a murderer who prided himself on his cold-bloodedness, might seem to us deviant, but in fact we all consistently view ourselves in a good light. Our true nature is selfconceit.

THE TRUTH OF WHAT LIES IN THE HEART

In Buddhism, people are evaluated three ways: by the heart, the mouth, and the body. Of these, the heart is the most important. A popular song in Japan contains this line: "Even dressed in rags, the heart is of brocade, lovelier by far than any flower."[102] Outward appearance matters nothing compared to what lies within. If someone says, "Your tie is twisted," the trouble is easily fixed, but to be told, "Your heart is twisted" is much harder to deal with. It is more hurtful because it insults our innermost core.

A similar pattern can be seen in American and British law, where murder and manslaughter are carefully distinguished: justifiable homicide and excusable homicide are non-culpable crimes, while first-degree murder—the willful, deliberate, and premeditated taking of another's life—is the most serious offense.

Why does the invisible heart, or mind, receive so much more emphasis than actions and utterances that we can see and hear? The answer is easy: the words of the mouth and the acts of the body are controlled by the thoughts of the mind. If the mind is a fire, then deeds and words are the sparks or emanations it gives off.

Once when the Russian writer Ivan Turgenev (1818–83) was penniless, a beggar came to his gates. Mortified that he had nothing to give, Turgenev ran out the front door, grasped the man's hand in his, and called him "Brother" with tears in his eyes. Later the beggar confessed that never in his life did he receive any gift so precious.

The Preamble to UNESCO's Constitution states that "since wars begin in the minds of men, it is in the minds of men that the defences of peace must be constructed." The statement acknowledges that the atrocity of war is rooted squarely in the human mind.

Buddhism always places priority on the workings of the mind or heart, just as firefighters focus on the origin of a fire.

Two Zen monks traveling about the country on a pilgrimage came to a small stream that was swollen from several days' rain. A lovely young woman was standing hesitantly at the water's edge, unable to bring herself to cross. "Here, let me help you," offered one of the monks, picking her up effortlessly and carrying her to the other side. Red with embarrassment, she murmured her thanks and slipped away. The other monk was scandalized that his companion would embrace a woman under any circumstances (their Zen sect had rigid rules forbidding contact with the opposite sex), and he maintained a strict discipline of silence the rest of the way.

As evening came on, the one who had carried the girl across the stream suggested that they stop somewhere for the night. The other replied coldly that he had no interest in lodging anywhere with a depraved monk. The first monk exclaimed, "What, are you still holding onto that girl?" and burst into laughter. Awakened to the depraved nature of his own thoughts, his companion could make no reply.

In this way, what lies in the heart or mind is most important.

And yet, evil though people's inmost thoughts may be, there is no prosecution or censure merely for thinking them. That is only natural, since all we can know of a person's thoughts are the sparks they set off in word or deed. There being no way to control the workings of another person's mind, thoughts are left to run rampant. The death poem of Ishikawa Goemon, a notorious thief of old Japan who was sentenced to die in a boiling cauldron, makes the point:

> Stony river![103]
> The sands of the shore
> may run out
> but the seeds that make men thieves
> will never be exhausted.

Buddhism teaches that the evil committed with the mouth or the body is nothing compared with the evil committed in the heart, since the thought is parent of both word and deed. That is why the mere contemplation of murder is no less evil than its commission.

Here is a poem of reflection by Genshin (942–1017), a learned monk whom Shinran revered as a patriarch of Pure Land faith:

> All night long
> I searched and searched
> for the Buddha's Way,
> only to arrive at last
> at the workings of my heart.

Your true self means the truth of what lies in your heart. What others say about you based on personal or social concepts of good and evil is not the truth; what you may think of yourself based on those same concepts is not the truth about you, either.

When the darkness of mind that hides the truth about oneself is dispelled, what is revealed?

In the next six chapters we will focus on the confessions of Shinran.

CHAPTER **14**

Revelation of the True Self

THE SEA OF LUST

A friend of ours was operated on for cataracts, a disease of the eye in which clouding of the lens causes vision to deteriorate—although today, artificial lenses have made possible dramatic recovery of sight. After the operation, our friend (who occasionally used to pick up centipedes, mistaking them for bits of string) looked into the mirror and got a jolt. It was like looking at her face under a microscope, she said. She took one look around her house and immediately started doing some spring-cleaning, appalled at the accumulation of dirt.

Once darkness of mind is dispelled, the nature of one's self is clearly revealed. This is called "revelation of the true self." Shinran wrote many confessions of his true nature:

> How grievous! As I, most foolish Shinran, am swallowed in the vast sea of lust and troubled by the great mountain of [desire for] fame and wealth, I neither rejoice in having been saved by Amida nor take pleasure in nearing the realization of true enlightenment. How shameful! How lamentable![104]

In other words, "Oh, how miserable I am! Drowning in the vast sea of lust, at the mercy of my greedy desire for reputation and riches, I am not the least happy that Amida has given me salvation or glad that I am coming closer to Buddha's enlightenment. I am thoroughly numb and unfeeling. How shameful, and how terribly sad."

We will explain the matter in greater detail beginning in Chapter 20, but "having been saved by Amida" and "nearing the realization of true enlightenment" both mean that the mind of ignorance concerning the afterlife (dark mind) has been destroyed and the purpose of living attained. Here Shinran makes plain both that he has been saved by Amida and that he is nearing the realization of true enlightenment; let us be clear that this revelation of the true self and this penitence belong only to those who share Shinran's knowledge and certainty of salvation.

Then what did he mean by the "vast sea of lust"? Śākyamuni Buddha said that when a man sees a beautiful woman, even though he knows that just below a thin layer of skin lies blood and uncleanness, his mind is ablaze with lewd thoughts.

> All men think lascivious thoughts, lighting up at sight of a female form, and indulging to their heart's content in obscene mental acts. Disgusted by his wife, and filled with hatred for her, a man steals lustful glances at other women in a continual agony of desire. Waves of lust rise high, swamping him again and again so that standing or sitting, he is never at ease.

The Blade-leaf Forest Hell mentioned in Buddhist scriptures is a portrayal of this human sea of lust. When a man goes to this hell, the first thing he notices is a huge tree reaching to the heavens, whose leaves, sharp as sword blades, emit fire. At the top of the tree is a woman he fancies, with a come-hither look on her face. She beckons to him. It is the sinner's former lover. In a fever of excitement and longing, he cannot sit still. Forgetting all else, he starts up the tree, only for a shower of blade-leaves to rain down upon him, rending his flesh and piercing his bones. Though he is covered head to toe in gore, his passion only mounts.

Finally managing to climb up beside the woman, he reaches out to embrace her with all his might, only for her to disappear like magic. Now she calls to him sweetly from the foot of the tree: "Darling, I came here out of love for you. Hurry and make love to me!"

There is something heartrending about the single-minded devotion of a man who would suffer so much to be with a woman. Now the flames of his love fan brighter still, and down the tree he goes. This time, the blade-leaves lying fallen on the ground, now pointed upwards, emit tongues of fire that penetrate every inch of his flesh and char his bones. His suffering defies description.

When he finally lands on the ground, the object of his desire is nowhere to be found: once again she calls to him from the treetop, writhing sensuously. Buddhism teaches that in this hell, the lover is condemned to climb up and down over and over, suffering continuously from unceasing lust.

Lovers part and long for one another, meet and become enemies inflicting pain on one another. With longings unfulfilled, they are consumed with desire; with longings fulfilled, their desire only doubles, eating them alive. The description aptly describes the torment of human sexual love and desire.

A man associated with rationality is the seventeenth-century thinker René Descartes, known as the father of modern philosophy. Yet that great philosopher had a child by his maid, making her an unwed mother.

Georg Wilhelm Friedrich Hegel (1770–1831), the German philosopher whose all-embracing work represents the summit of modern philosophy, wrote his first major work, *Phenomenology of Spirit*, at the age of thirty-six. While working on it, he carried on an affair with his married landlady, and fathered an illegitimate child. Fearful of losing his professorship at the University in Jena, one month later he fled the city, leaving the infant with a friend and promising his lover he would marry her if her husband died. Yet four years later he wed a woman twenty years his junior, from an old patrician family.

Karl Marx (1818–83), author of one of the main currents of contemporary philosophy, was critical of Hegel's idealism, but shared his fallibility. While appealing to workers of the world to overthrow the bourgeois yoke, he married an aristocrat and then impregnated her maid. Not only that, he pressured his accommodating friend Friedrich Engels (1820–95) into acknowledging the child as his own.

The image of human beings drowning in a sea of lust too vast to swim across captures our real state all too accurately.

> Blind passions are thick within me.
> Like dust, they fill my every corner.
> My love for those who accommodate me,
> my hate for those who oppose me,
> are like lofty peaks and high mountains.[105]

To paraphrase: "Poisonous flames of anger and desire are set off throughout my body. I love and draw near to those who accommodate me, I despise and keep at arm's length those who oppose me. The will to do so is high and vast within me, exactly like soaring mountain peaks."

Shinran's words express the deep contrition of a man who is solemnly aware of his heavy burden of worldly passions and sinfulness. Nor is Shinran the only one ever to be submerged in the vast sea of lust and passion.

CHAPTER **15**

The Universal Desire for Fame and Fortune

OUR HUNGER FOR RECOGNITION

> How grievous! As I … am swallowed in the vast sea of lust
> and troubled by the great mountain of [desire for] fame and
> wealth …[106]

We have examined the "vast sea of lust" that Shinran speaks of here;
now, what of the "great mountain of [desire for] fame and wealth"?
Fame means the desire for honor: we want to be well thought of, to be
praised for our ability, style, sweetness, or looks; we do not want to be
disliked or to have people speak ill of us. Wealth means the desire for
profit: we want all the money and things we can possibly acquire.

Shinran describes himself as a wretched fellow drowning in the vast
sea of his raging desires, at the mercy day and night of his towering lust
for fame and wealth, without a scrap of thanksgiving or contrition. The
words ring with the conviction of true penitence.

Alfred Adler (1870–1937), the Austrian psychiatrist who founded the
school of individual psychology, suggested that the basic driving force of
human behavior is a "striving for superiority." Our inborn desire to demonstrate superiority is reinforced by others' tendency to praise us for
winning and look down on us for losing. In today's fierce struggle for
existence, competition goes on heating up at work and at school. The
Japanese education system is sometimes viewed with admiration and
envy by those in other countries, but in fact, thanks to its relentless ex-

aminations, competition has wormed its way even into the lives of kindergarten pupils there, who often attend cram school and take lessons in everything from thinking skills to art, in order to get into an exclusive elementary school—seen as a stepping-stone toward a prestigious career.

Diligently we strive to claw our way to the top, so that we may lord it over others and look down on them. We take pride in our wealth, and flaunt our intellectual and physical prowess. If we lack any particular superiority of our own, we brag instead about our children, our workplace, or our country. In prisons, it is said that inmates even develop a sense of superiority based on the number of their previous offenses.

This hunger for the prestige of winning has its price. In Japan, school bullying is a perennial problem that has driven a distressing number of young people to suicide. Often it seems to arise out of envy at the superiority of a few. Students whose grades are markedly good, or who are especially attractive, make easy targets. A friend tells the following story about his high school days:

"My best buddy was particularly good at English, and he inevitably outscored me on tests. Only once did I beat him, and that was the time he came down with acute pneumonia and had to stay home the day of the test. Usually the two of us goofed around and laughed together, but even so, when I heard he'd gotten sick I was jubilant. The memory is painful to me now. Envying my friend his success, I betrayed our friendship with utter unconcern—all the while wanting more than anything else to be trusted. What gall!"

The father of master swordsman Miyamoto Musashi (1584–1645), Munisai, was so envious of his son's talent that he followed him with intent to kill. The lust for honor causes sparks to fly even between parent and child. Among friends or between master and pupil, conflict is even more likely.

While Nobel Prize–winner Bertrand Russell was teaching mathematics, Ludwig Wittgenstein (1889–1951), who would later become one of the giants of twentieth-century philosophy, signed up for his course. Only a year or two later, Wittgenstein began to heap severe criticism on his mentor. The humiliation of this was apparently too much for Russell, who took to hurling abusive language at his pupil, and expunged his name from certain of his writings.

A rival is someone who spurs one to be one's best, and to whom one therefore owes a great debt; nevertheless, we hate our rivals, and do all we can to hurt them and bring them crashing down. This too is a by-product of our hunger for fame and honor.

THE DEPTHS OF HUMAN DECEIT

Even the world of science, which presents a calm and pristine image to outsiders, is aswirl with lust for fame and honor. James D. Watson, 1962 winner of a Nobel Prize for researches elucidating the structure of DNA, wrote graphically in his book *The Double Helix* about questionable methods he used, including stealing peeks at classified information through deception and concealing his results from rival scientists. Yet Watson failed to see anything untoward in such behavior, writing, "It was certainly better to imagine myself becoming famous than maturing into a stifled academic who had never risked a thought."[107] Similarly, Sir Isaac Newton (1642–1727), the father of modern science, fought furiously in a long, ugly dispute with Baron Gottfried Wilhelm Leibniz (1646–1716) over which man deserved credit for the discovery of differential and integrated calculus.

Countless men and women have come to an ignominious end, crushed beneath the "great mountain of fame and wealth." In November 2000, a prominent Japanese archeologist was exposed as a fraud. Video cameras caught him stealthily burying pieces of stoneware from another excavation site with his own hands. His claim to have discovered Stone Age objects dating as far back as six hundred thousand years was proven a fabrication, and archaeological studies in Japan suffered an enormous setback. Time and time again, this man had published results pushing back the earliest limits of Japan's Paleolithic age, completely refiguring the contours of prehistory. His uncanny ability to locate key artifacts had earned him the nickname "God's hands."

The aesthetics of death that make us wish to end life in a blaze of glory are one more expression of the desire for fame and honor.

To hang onto transitory bits of comfort, we deceive ourselves and others. We hold others in contempt while seeming to praise them, and we seem to humble ourselves while taking pride in the depths of our humility.

Lying contest:
old woman who wants to die,
daughter-in-law who stops her

We brazenly lie, and paint ourselves as virtuous. The mother-in-law in this anonymous satirical poem has not the slightest intention of dying, but because she doesn't care for her son's wife's attitude, she tries to gain the upper hand by saying out loud that she wants to die. The son's wife is no fool. Knowing perfectly well what game the old lady is playing, she thinks to herself, "Drop dead then, why don't you?" but on the surface she plays the part of a devoted daughter-in-law. "You are the mainstay of this family. You have to live on in good health for many years to come, Mother, or what will become of us?" Both women are lying in their teeth, while sounding utterly sincere.

"The heart and the mouth do not agree; there is truth neither in what people say, nor in what they think." These words of Śākyamuni from the Larger Sutra of Infinite Life unmask human deceit and faithlessness. The things we say with our mouths are different from the thoughts we think in our hearts. Neither one is true. We are full of lies and deception.

At the foolish praise of foolish people we walk on air, while the taunts of children send our spirits plunging. The Buddha's words bring home the sadness of our state, slaves as we are to the desire for fame and honor.

DEMON GOLD

An eighty-year-old man lived with his eldest son, an executive in a large company. The old man had not been feeling well for some time, and a series of tests disclosed liver cancer. Assuming the end was near, the son urged his father to go into the hospital for surgery, while at the same time preparing a list of people to notify in case of death. For her part, the son's wife took the old man's seal and closed out his savings account. But the old man rebounded after the operation, and was soon released from the hospital. Surprise and disappointment were writ large on the faces of the son and his wife, without a trace of guilt. Heartless greed made them value the old man's wealth above his life.

> At the moment of death, nothing one has previously relied on, whether wife and child or money and treasure, will accompany one. At the end of the mountain road of death, one must cross the river all alone.[108]

This means that when we die, nothing we have turned to for support until then will be of any avail, including family and possessions. Torn from them all, we must leave this world unaided.

Even if we live a long life, it likely will not last a hundred years, and when we go, we take nothing with us. The words of the renowned priest Rennyo above leave no room for disagreement, and yet we cannot escape our insatiable desires. Even if gold rained from the skies, we would not be able to gather enough to satisfy our strong greed.

The Japanese novelist Kan Kikuchi (1888–1948) declared, "Most adversity can be swept away with money." Then and now, many people would agree with him. They are scandalous lovers of demon gold, willing to do anything for its sake.

In November 2005, in Massachusetts, a radio personality was charged with first-degree murder in the death of his wife the previous year. He was accused of spiking her Gatorade with antifreeze over a four-month period so he could collect on a $250,000 life insurance policy. Hearing that someone could watch dispassionately as his spouse slowly suffered and died, we may shudder with revulsion, but cases of murder for insurance money are by no means rare.

In 2002, a forty-three-year-old nurse in Nara, Japan, was found guilty of attempted murder for giving poisoned tea to her fifteen-year-old daughter, her own flesh and blood. A life insurance policy worth thirty million yen (roughly US$300,000) had been taken out on the girl. The mother was also placed under suspicion of having murdered two other children three years earlier—a boy, then fifteen, and a girl, then nine—using the same technique; on their deaths she had collected twenty million yen (roughly US$200,000) in insurance money.

A flea makes flea waste, an elephant, elephant waste. As people increase in status, the scale of their misdeeds increases likewise. How many high government officials, ministers of state, and prime ministers have been sent to prison for acceptance of a bribe, to end their days in humiliation? How many people have watched edifices that had been painstakingly built be crushed to bits against the mountain of desire for fame and wealth, so that nothing remains but regret? Such people serve as mirrors for our own greedy, grasping ways.

We are as stolid as swine when it comes to the interests of other people, but the minute our own profit is involved, we are all attention. If someone is standing in the way of our desires, even a relative or a benefactor, we will push him down and stab him in the heart with never a second thought or a second's pity.

Here is a story with a moral.

Three thieves stole a lot of money and made off with it to the top of a mountain. As they started to divide it, one of them got greedy and thought of a plan. "Wait," he said cunningly. "Let's have something to eat first. I'll go find us some grub." And off he went to town. The other two thieves were hungry, so that was fine with them.

The first thief went to town and bought some buns. After eating his fill, he injected poison into the rest. He was plotting to murder his companions out of greed. While he was gone, the other two laid their own evil designs. They agreed to finish their companion off and split the money evenly.

When the first thief returned, he threw down the bag of buns and said, "Help yourselves. I already ate." And then, laughing inside, he went off to relieve himself by the edge of a cliff. Seeing their chance, the other two crept up behind him and gave him a shove, sending him tumbling into the valley below. "So much for him. Now let's eat, and then split the take." They died side by side. All that remained on the mountaintop was the bag of money.

> I peer
> into the depths of the abyss
> where I must fall—
> ah, how unfathomable,
> the pit of my desires.[109]

We want a good reputation, wealth and treasure, this and that, more, more, more … We suffer constantly in our pursuit of ever more fame and wealth, and in the end we die, leaving all behind. The story of the three thieves encapsulates human folly.

ENDLESS SELF-INTEREST

A troupe of performing monkeys, spurred on by the showman's cries, put on an excellent act. One viewer was so impressed that, without thinking, she tossed them a tangerine as reward. The results were disastrous. Everything the monkeys had learned went out the window, and they converged on the lone tangerine in a mad scramble. As they fought and bit each other, frantic to gain possession, the act was ruined.

Both the desire for fame and the desire for wealth are selfish in nature. When we are tossed the tangerine of honor and wealth, all the ethics and culture we ever knew, acquired, or understood go by the board as our true nature comes to the fore. A cup of the water of reason cannot extinguish the roaring inferno of our desire for fame and wealth.

An example of this happened towards the end of the Pacific War, when a Japanese transport ship forced to sail without escort was sunk in a torpedo attack. Thousands of soldiers thrown into the sea made a rush for the few lifeboats available, which quickly filled to the limit. If even one too many came on board, all would sink—yet those in the water kept on coming, clinging desperately to the edge of the boat. The men on board took up their bayonets and, one after another, severed the hands clutching the gunwale. Soldiers whose hands were cut off at the wrist disappeared into the blood-red waters, glaring balefully at the heartless killers who had been their comrades in arms.

"I saved my life, but my soul is lost forever": This is the confession of one soldier who returned home after a hairbreadth escape.

"The Spider's Thread," a classic short story by Ryunosuke Akutagawa, brilliantly captures the true nature of humanity's selfish greed. In it, Buddha takes pity on Kandata, a sinner suffering the torments of the damned in Hell. Recalling that the notorious thief had once spared the life of a spider, Buddha lowers a spider's thread down into Hell as a means for him to escape. At first the plan works perfectly. Kandata grabs hold and starts to shinny his way up, seeking escape. On tiring, he pauses, looks down, and makes a shocking discovery: suspended below him is a multitude of sinners, all hanging from the same thread, aiming to share in his good fortune. Fearful the thread will break, Kandata yells for them to get off. Only then does the thread snap, and all plummet back together into Hell.

"Kandata's hard heart, that cared nothing for others as long as he himself was saved, plunged him back into Hell. Ah, he was truly beyond salvation ..." The deep sigh of the Buddha seems to fill our ears.

But it is not only Kandata who was given up on as "truly beyond salvation." There is a Kandata living deep in the heart of each of us.

CHAPTER 16

The Evil Within

FOR ALL CREATURES, DEATH MEANS SUFFERING

One need not be an expert on Charles Darwin's theory of evolution or Herbert Spencer's writings on "survival of the fittest" to see that the law of the jungle is a stark reality. Some people would argue that this is a natural state of affairs: "The only way we can live is by taking the lives of other creatures, since the continuity of life depends on other life for sustenance. Only when we boldly engage in the taking of life do our day-to-day lives brighten up. Offering consolation is for decrepit old people to do; feeling pity is a retreat from true life." That is certainly one way of looking at things, but taken to extremes it would mean putting the seal of approval on despotism and terrorism.

We take the eating of meat for granted, and yet animals do not regard themselves as existing for our sake, nor do they see their sacrifice as natural and inevitable. Death means suffering for animals as surely as it does for us. Why does a fish flop around on the deck of a fishing boat, and why does a chicken beat its wings as its neck is being wrung? Because they are suffering, surely. To dismiss such suffering on the grounds that it is necessary in order for us to live, as if only human life were precious, is surely the height of selfish arrogance. The animals that we kill doubtless go to their deaths cursing us for our cruelty. They must feel all the bitterness of a human condemned to death on a false charge.

In April 2000, we heard an unusual crime reported on the radio in Japan. Several men were arrested on charges of abducting and killing two women, who had been found burned beyond recognition. The men had apparently not killed their victims and then incinerated the bodies for concealment, as one might suppose, but, according to a confession made by one of the men, poured gasoline over the two women while they were still alive, and literally burned them to death. Our first reaction was, "How could anyone do anything so cruel?" Then we were brought up short, realizing we are party to a similar cruelty. What about the way we ourselves consume grilled meat with gusto? (From the perspective of Buddhism, the two acts are equally heinous. In the words of Ralph Waldo Emerson: "You have just dined, and, however scrupulously the slaughter-house is concealed in the graceful distance of miles, there is complicity."[110]) Can we truly say we would never, under any circumstances, commit the other crime as well?

In the United States, over one hundred thousand cattle are slaughtered per day. A visitor to a meat processing plant in Denver reports that hundreds of cattle are herded into a narrow passageway with concrete walls, at the end of which is a machine that delivers a stunning blow to the head of each animal in turn, with the push of a button. Some animals panic and try to get away, but they are hampered by the cattle pressing up behind them, and all are brought down in the end. To satisfy the human appetite for beef, this scenario is reenacted all over the country—all over the world—day after day after day. Nor is it only cattle that are killed. How many animal lives have been sacrificed, all told?

SAVING ONE LIFE AND TAKING OTHERS

The fairy tale "Urashima Taro" is well known in Japan. One day Urashima Taro, a fisherman, goes to the beach and finds children tormenting a sea turtle. He lectures them that they must be kind to animals, but the children do not listen. In the end he buys the sea turtle from them, takes it out to sea in his boat, and sets it free. A few days later, as he is fishing in his boat, the turtle he rescued comes by with an offer to take him to the fabled Dragon Palace underneath the sea. Taro agrees, and ends up staying there for some time, enjoying the company of Princess Otohime and being treated to all manner of fine foods and entertainments.

Children told this story are encouraged to grow up to be tender-hearted, like the main character. Yet how many children (or their parents, for that matter) stop to think about the fishing pole over Taro's shoulder? It is nothing more nor less than an instrument for taking the lives of fish, which Taro goes on doing. If Urashima Taro were a true protector of animals, he should have broken his fishing pole in two and thrown it away. Someone who casually takes the lives of tens of thousands of creatures on the one hand, and then tries to pass himself off as compassionate and virtuous on the other by saving the life of a single creature of a different genus, is a transparent imposter.

Yet Urashima Taro's livelihood depends on his fishing pole. To throw it away would be a form of suicide. Herein lies his limitation as a would-be man of virtue: though capable of saving a single life, he cannot live without taking the lives of countless others. This is his unalterable predicament. His story is in fact a portrait of the human state.

In October 1972, a small plane bearing members of a college rugby team from Uruguay and their friends and acquaintances crashed on a frozen mountainside in the Andes. More than half of the passengers survived the crash, but they had no food, water, or warm clothing. Their situation became even grimmer when the rescue search was called off. Yet seventy-one days later, sixteen people were rescued alive in what became known around the world as the "miracle of the Andes." Scattered around the fuselage of the crashed airplane were human bones stripped neatly of meat, and empty skulls.

Towards the end of World War II, Japanese soldiers in the South Pacific would tell each other on parting, "Watch out you don't get eaten." On the brink of starvation, Japanese troops had changed into cannibalistic savages. In the beginning, the practice was limited to stripping flesh from the thighs of the dead, but eventually soldiers began killing each other for food. Young, well-muscled men were especially targeted. The victim would be tied to a log and surrounded by fifteen or sixteen men squatting in a circle, helping themselves to the flesh as it roasted.

Such stories send a shiver of horror down the spine, but what if we had been there? What would we have done? Have we any right to pass judgment?

Whenever a celebrity is involved in a scandal, or some unprecedented crime takes place, the media go into overdrive, offering a chorus of shocked criticism: "It's unthinkable!" "What kind of a person would do such a thing?" and so on. They are taking the perspective of the victim, of course, yet one cannot help wondering—is there anyone so infallible that the possibility of committing any given crime is truly zero? Analytical psychologist Carl Jung wrote, "The evil that … undoubtedly dwells within [man] is of gigantic proportions."[111]

Under the right conditions, I, Shinran, would do anything.[112]

As Shinran confesses here, the self is a potential brute capable of any act, however arbitrary and horrific. Shinran cannot point to any act as one of which he is incapable.

ENJOYING THE MISERY OF OTHERS

When our desires are thwarted, we become angry. Especially if we are scolded in front of other people, we feel a sense of humiliation that remains with us till our dying day. The Chinese character for "anger" is written with two elements, one meaning "heart" and the other "that fellow." We are quick to blame others in anger and frustration, complaining that "it's all that fellow's fault," and "if only he weren't around, everything would be fine." We are only too ready to dispatch someone standing in our way. Anger is a raging fire that stains us bright red; we throw all our learning and culture into the cauldron, not caring if the flames reduce everything in sight to ashes.

In one of the most celebrated episodes in Japanese history, Asano Naganori (1667–1701), the brash young lord of Ako (today's Hyogo Prefecture), was slighted by a shogunal representative, whom he subsequently attacked in Edo Castle in a fit of rage. As a result of this serious breach of order, Asano was ordered to commit *seppuku*, or ritual suicide.

His rash action thus cost him not only a wealthy fief but his own life—
nor was that the end of the matter: about two years later, his loyal samurai
retainers avenged their master's death and disgrace by killing the man
who had provoked him. All forty-six were then ordered to commit
seppuku, and did so. Ever since, this story has been told and retold as an
admirable example of loyalty and samurai ethics. From another perspective, however, it shows the destructive power of anger.

That power is no less strong now. Every day, newspapers run stories of
distraught young men who throw their lives away as, spurned by a lover,
they turn to stalking, then murder.

Directed toward a weak opponent, anger takes the form of reckless
lashing out; directed toward someone stronger than oneself, it settles
into deep animosity. When anger cannot be expressed directly, it often
takes the form of envy and ill will. As the saying goes in Japanese, "Lately
things have been going badly for me—especially after my neighbor's
new storehouse went up." When we are distracted by a run of bad luck,
the success of others rankles. We end up praying for misfortune to strike
our neighbors. Amicable friendship goes by the board.

A mere glimpse of our beloved talking on close terms to someone of
the opposite sex is enough to make us feel jealous. So fearsome and
loathsome are naked jealousy and envy that Shinran sadly likened the
heart out of which they grow to a "venomous snake or scorpion."[113]

Satirist Ambrose Bierce (1842–1914?) wrote in *The Devil's Dictionary*
that happiness is "an agreeable sensation arising from contemplating the
misery of another." The Germans even have a word, *schadenfreude*,
which means "delight in others' misfortune." We enjoy seeing someone
caught in a shower with no umbrella, we laugh at someone frightened by
a barking dog, and we are tickled by the sight of a well-dressed woman
on the verge of tears after being spattered with mud by a passing car. On
our way to see a fire, we are disappointed to hear it has been put out.
The Japanese have a saying that "away from home, the bigger the fire,
the greater the fun." Likewise, to "watch a fire on the opposite bank"
means to look on others' troubles with unconcern, as having nothing to
do with oneself. To take pleasure in such tragedy is indecent, we know,
yet despite ourselves we are morbidly fascinated, enjoying the spectacle

and incapable of working up any sadness. What does it say about people that viewer ratings and sales of tabloid newspapers never fail to go up when some big scandal or atrocity occurs?

Reports of another's good fortune, whether it be a promotion, a wedding, or a new home, leave us resentful. In contrast, on hearing that someone has failed in business, gotten a divorce, or suffered some other misfortune, we secretly smirk. What if our inmost thoughts were laid bare for all to see? People would surely call us monsters and flee our presence.

> Therefore, I am neither good nor wise, nor do I have any intention of being diligent. My spirit is one of nothing but indolence, and inside I am nothing but empty, deceitful, and fawning at all times. It has been impressed upon me that there is no truth in me.[114]

To paraphrase: "This is the kind of man that I, Shinran, am. As you see, I am neither a good man nor a wise one. I only want to be lazy, and I make no effort to be upstanding. My heart is empty. I am a capital liar who worries constantly about what other people think of me. The one thing I am certain of is the complete lack of truth in me."

Shinran's true self is truly one of no truth. Who but Shinran could make this stark declaration?

CHAPTER 17

Poisoned Good

DEMANDING GRATITUDE

> My evil nature knows no end.
> My mind is like a venomous snake or scorpion.
> The good acts I perform are tainted with poison,
> and so they are called false and empty practices.[115]

"What am I to do with myself? My mind, like a venomous snake or scorpion, shows no sign of stopping. Since my every act is polluted with this mind, naturally in the eyes of Buddha the good I do is poisoned."

What does Shinran mean by "good acts … tainted with poison"?

If I take my neighbor a present of homemade cookies without receiving any thanks, I am indignant. Soon I start telling myself I should not have bothered taking cookies to such an ingrate. The next time I see her, I fish openly for compliments, saying something like, "You know those cookies I gave you the other day—I'm afraid they didn't turn out very well, did they?"

Long ago, a Zen monk ventured out one raw winter day and saw, huddled beneath a bridge, a shivering beggar. The monk removed his robe and tossed it to the beggar. The beggar put the robe on, giving the monk a single glance, and said nothing. The monk couldn't resist calling out, "How's that? A little warmer now, eh?" The reply was swift. "Of course it is, what do you think? Don't ask silly questions. Be glad you're the one who's got robes to give away." The monk, who'd been expecting effusive thanks, was shamefaced to find himself seen through.

Everyone in Japan is familiar with the tale of the Tongue-Cut Sparrow. An old man had a pet sparrow he was very fond of. One day when the old man was out, the sparrow ate up all his wife's starch. The old woman was so angry that she took out her scissors and snipped off the sparrow's tongue, rendering it mute. The poor sparrow flew off in tears. When the old man came home and heard what had happened, he was appalled at his wife's cruelty, and set off to find off his dear little friend. After a long, hard search, he finally did find her, and stayed the afternoon, happy just to be reunited. When it was time to go home, the sparrow offered him his choice between two trunks to take home, one large and one small. Without hesitation, the old man picked the smaller one because it was lighter and easier to carry. When he got it home, it turned out to be full of gold and jewels.

The old woman promptly set out to claim her reward for "all she'd done to look after that sparrow." She had her heart set on treasure, so when she was offered the same choice as her husband, she picked the larger trunk. It turned out to be full of all kinds of scary animals and monsters—representations of her own calculating, greedy heart.

Emperor Wu (464–549) of Liang is famous in Chinese history as a devout Buddhist ruler who erected countless temples and pagodas, making great contributions to the spread of Buddhism in his country. When the priest Bodhidharma came from India at the venerable age of 120, Emperor Wu entertained him in person as a state guest. The first chance he got, he said eagerly to his guest: "Since becoming emperor, I have overseen the building of countless temples and pagodas. I have firmly protected monks and nuns, and done all I could to further the spread of Buddhism throughout the land. How much merit have I accumulated, do you think?"

"None!" thundered Bodhidharma.

"How can you say that?" said Emperor Wu, offended.

His guest said firmly, "Yours is nothing but false virtue and poisoned good."

The good that we do gives off a terrible stink, since we pat ourselves on the back and look down arrogantly on others, who we feel do not do nearly as much good as we do.

Reader's Card

Thank you for purchasing this book.
We would appreciate if you would fill out the following questionnaire and return it to us. We will use the information you provide as our inspiration for the next publication.

Book Title: *YOU WERE BORN FOR A REASON*

1. When and where did you buy this book?
   Date: Place:
2. How did you discover this book?
   ☐Heard about it from friend/present.
   ☐Saw it in the bookstore. (Name of the store:)
   ☐Saw ad in the paper or magazine. (Name of media:)
   ☐Got a bookmark of this book. (How did you get it?   )
   ☐Saw it on the Internet.
   ☐Others (   )
3. What motivated you to buy this book?

.

Name:

Age:

Sex: ☐Male   ☐Female

Occupation:

Street:

City:

State: Zip: Country:

Phone: Fax:

E-mail:

THE IMPOSSIBILITY OF DOING GOOD

We tell ourselves we want to help others and "make a difference." That of course is easier said than done.

A philanthropist started sending New Year's rice-cakes to impoverished families. The first few years he received letters of thanks, but eventually the letters dropped off—and instead he started hearing complaints: the rice-cakes this year came later than usual, or they were too small, people said. Disgusted, he quit sending any.

The pattern repeats endlessly, in others and in oneself: we think we are doing good out of the kindness of our heart, only to become irked at the recipient's failure to respond with a compliment or a "simple thank-you." Generosity changes to indignation: "After all I've done for you!" In no time, we are resolving never to lift a finger to help so-and-so again. The ideographs for "hypocrite" in Japanese mean "someone who does good while saying it is for the benefit of others." We know that the joy of giving is greater than the joy of receiving; the trouble is, we can never totally forget that we gave.

If we give money to the destitute and receive no thanks, we take offense, our anger increasing in direct proportion to the amount given. This is because to our minds, larger gifts represent greater goodness: a hundred-dollar donation is outweighed by one of a thousand dollars, a thousand-dollar donation by one of a million. But from the perspective of Buddha, who sees the tiniest speck of evil, the greater the good a person thinks he has done, the greater the evil harbored in the act. Buddhism teaches that human beings are incapable of true goodness.

The Buddhist philosopher Nāgārjuna (ca. 150–250) expressed the reality of human goodness this way: "Even if you pour two or three jugs of boiling water on a frozen pond four miles around, the next day, the ice there will swell up."[116] In other words, boiling water may have power to melt ice, but overnight it too will freeze. In the same way, human goodness is overwhelmed by our overriding capacity for evil.

One may well ask, if doing good with pure motives is impossible, is it then preferable to be cold and unfeeling? Is not the ability to feel pity valuable? Should we never try to do anyone a good turn? Will not saying these things only encourage people to be more self-indulgent?

Let there be no misunderstanding. The sort of person under consideration here—one who feels pity and compassion for those in unfortunate circumstances and takes action to help them, only to be brought up short by the realization that his benevolence is tainted by ugly pride—is by definition one whose heart is sincerely set on doing good; otherwise, he would be incapable of such a deep realization. The more we try to become good, the more we see that our "evil nature knows no end," and the more we are driven to repent and to strive to overcome our natural bent for evil. Even then we are dismayed by the ugly self-interest that continues to masquerade as virtue, infecting our sincerest efforts. The lying, deceitful nature that Shinran grieved over was his true self, revealed to him after the lifting of his dark mind.

> Since I myself have neither a dab of pity nor an iota of compassion, I cannot presume to seek others' happiness.[117]

In other words, "I once thought I had a little pity for my fellow man, a little desire to help, but that was an illusion. I, Shinran, do not have a shred of compassion."

The pain and sorrow of this lament could only belong to someone who had seen clearly into the true nature of his being.

CHAPTER 18

Confronting the Self

> In all human beings, at all times, thoughts of greed and lust continually defile any goodness of heart. Thoughts of anger and hatred continually consume the desire to follow Buddha's way. Even if one acts and practices with urgency, as though sweeping fire from one's head, everything that one does is called "poisoned good and its accumulation," and "false and deceitful practice." It is not called "true good."[118]

This passage from *Teaching, Practice, Faith, Enlightenment* may be rephrased as follows: We think only of our own advantage; our hearts are stirred only by the desire to eat, to drink, to play, to enjoy leisure, to sleep. We seek sexual gratification, we long for honor, we chase after money: our desires spread out without limit. "What a fool I am," we say, but if anyone else calls us a fool, we bridle. We don't really consider ourselves fools at all. We think and we say what suits our own convenience, we have a high opinion of ourselves, and all we want is praise. In this way, human goodness is universally tainted with filthy desire, frightful anger, and hideous envy. Anyone whose hair caught on fire would drop everything to snuff the fire out at once; even if we try to do good with that same intensity, we are incapable of pure good. All we produce is hypocrisy and lies.

And yet even someone who takes his wickedness very much to heart does not think he is all bad. Somewhere inside, he gives himself credit for reflecting on his actions and being ashamed of himself. Novelist Hiroyuki Itsuki (1932–), a self-professed fan of Shinran's, has had this to say about the human condition:

> Are human beings really all that great, all that remarkable? Is being ashamed of one's humanity a negative and shameful way to think? I say no. Never mind the rest of the human race; just looking at myself, I cannot get over what a wretched creature I am. I think only how to defend myself, and have no real love for others. Unable to control my desires, I am wedded to material things. I live in fear of poverty, illness, and death. Stories in the newspapers and on TV of overseas disasters, civil wars, famine, and poverty cause me only a moment's pain. My will is weak and I soon go back on my decisions.[119]

Itsuki's declaration of his shame seems to show commendable insight and soul-searching. It is hard for any of us to think that we are incapable of shame, and that our best efforts are only hypocrisy and lies, but that is the truth.

LACK OF ANY SHAME OR PENITENCE

Now let us hear what Shinran has to say.

> Impenitent toward others,
> unashamed in my heart,
> I lack a mind of truth;
> but because I have received Amida's Name,
> virtue fills the ten directions.[120]

The first two lines mean having no sense of shame, feeling neither any penitence toward others nor any shame in the depths of one's heart for the evil one commits. The verse may be paraphrased thus: "I erupt in anger if anyone criticizes me for being steeped in selfish desire, nor do I think myself a bad fellow in the least. There is no trace of truth in me.

But having received from Amida the crystallized virtue of the cosmos (Namu Amida Butsu), I am filled with truth and overcome with joy."

Blessings that call for rejoicing bring forth no joy in him; he is neither grateful nor repentant. One who is dead to shame can never be brought to shame; thus, insensible to shame and blind to his own wrongdoing, Shinran looks down on others and throws his weight around with arrogance and disdain. Where no amount of prostration and apology could suffice, he is brazenly indifferent, without a speck of penitence. His heart is cold and dead.

Once made to see he was the vilest and most depraved of sinners, beyond all hope of redemption, Shinran stated with tears of anguish, "I am incapable of doing any good at all, and so Hell is my eternal dwelling-place."[121] This is the bottom of despair.

Consciousness of being "impenitent toward others, unashamed in my heart"—knowledge that comes only from the revelation of one's absolutely evil and shameless self—is in itself the greatest state of penitence and shame there could be. It is appropriately known as "matchless penitence."

An Italian nursery story illustrates the difference. In the deep of night a candle burned in a mountain cabin, convinced it was as bright as anything could be. Then came an oil lamp, with similar delusions of grandeur. Next came an electric light, arrogant and full of self-conceit, but so bright that the candle and the lamp could only hang their heads. Then when morning came, the sun arose in the eastern sky. Thoroughly eclipsed, the candle, the oil lamp, and the electric light all went dark. That was the end of their boasting.

When X-rays are taken, all people, whether pretty or ugly, rich or poor, male or female, old or young, are reduced to nothing but a stark chain of bones. In the same way, when our darkness of mind is dispelled, we see ourselves clearly as forever lost, hopelessly evil, impenitent toward others and unashamed at heart. This is the revelation of the true self.

> The sentient beings are filled with blind passion. By nature they lack a mind of truth or purity, their thoughts being entirely evil and wicked.[122]

In other words, we human beings are by our very nature given solely to vice, and there is no truth or purity in us. This fundamental reality is something that can never be revealed without our plunging to the very bottom of Hell's abyss.

CHAPTER 19

The Real Meaning of Evil

One of the most celebrated statements attributed to Shinran is this: "If even a good person will attain salvation, all the more so will an evil person."[123] This doctrine is often summed up in the phrase *akunin shoki*, meaning "the evil person is the true object of salvation." Then what is an "evil person"? Many people may envision the inhuman sort of person who kills in cold blood without a flicker of remorse—but is that all Shinran meant by "evil person"? Let us take a look at another statement he made.

REVELATION OF THE TRUE SELF

> I am, now, a foolish being imbued with evil and caught in the cycle of birth and death, constantly submerged and constantly wandering for all these countless aeons without ever a chance for liberation: this is clearly revealed to me.[124]

This statement means, "I have come to see my present self clearly as the vilest and most depraved of sinners, suffering throughout eternity with absolutely no possibility of salvation."

Because this passage is so essential to an understanding of Shinran's thought, at the risk of belaboring it, let us go over it carefully to be sure that we grasp its import. Here "I" does not refer to the self in the past or future. Rather, Shinran is professing that when he was shown clearly the nature of his present self, his past and his future were likewise illuminated. The words "I am, now, a foolish being imbued with evil and caught in the cycle of birth and death" mean that his present self has been revealed to him as such a person. The moment that happens, he sees simultaneously his past ("constantly submerged and constantly wandering for all these countless aeons") and his future ("without ever a chance for liberation"). "Constantly submerged and constantly wandering for all these countless aeons" means that he has been suffering continually for ages past without beginning, and "without ever a chance for liberation" means that he has absolutely no prospect of salvation, that Hell is his "eternal dwelling-place."

Some readers may question how it is possible for anyone to know the worlds of the past or future. According to Shinran, since the present embraces both the past from time immemorial and the future without end, to see the present clearly is to know the entire past and future at once. The present is the key that unlocks the past and the future.

The following story clearly shows the interrelatedness of the present and the future.

A learned man of some note came to town to lecture on the evils of drink and preach the wisdom of abstinence. A townsman passionately fond of drinking marched into the lecture hall, indignant that anyone would wish to impugn one of life's great pleasures. But the more he heard the more he learned, and slowly, against his will, he found himself being won over. Suddenly relenting, he resolved to become a teetotaler. When the lecture was over, he went up to the learned man and told him the whole story, finally asking him to write something to commemorate his resolution.

"What shall I write?"

"How about, 'No Drinking Till the Day I Die?'"

"That sounds awfully hard. Why not make it just for today?"

Scarcely able to believe his ears, the man leaned forward to make sure he'd heard right. "Just for today? Is that good enough?"

"Certainly. Just give up drinking for today. That will do."

The man took home the paper with the words "No Drinking Just for Today" on it, and stuck it on the wall. Then he took out his watch and waited expectantly for tomorrow. As night came on and the hour of midnight approached, he got out a big jug of wine and pulled it close with anticipation. As the clock struck twelve, he picked up the jug, got ready to take a long drink, and then glanced over at the wall. A wave of disappointment struck him. "Oh no!" he cried out. "'No drinking just for today,' all over again!"

In fact, "just for today" means the same as "till the day I die." That truth came home to the man, and he never took another drink as long as he lived.

When "this year" is over, it is "this year" again. When "today" ends, it is "today" again. Time stretches on from ages past into the never-ending future, an endless succession of moments in the present: "now," "now," "now" … Because the present moment embraces the eternal past and the eternal future, philosophers through the ages have spoken of it as the "eternal Now."

DEATH COMES IN AN INSTANT

We have indicated that "the mind of darkness" means "the mind ignorant of the afterlife." People tend to think of the world after death as something to face thirty or fifty years down the road, but is that true? If we die tonight, it begins tonight. Or it could begin even sooner: an hour from now, or a minute.

In the huge earthquake of 1995 that devastated the city of Kobe, some young people died while studying at their desks. Each day, around the world many people lose their lives in traffic accidents and other unforeseen events. We cannot tell when we may be thrust into the next life.

Śākyamuni Buddha taught, "The outgoing breath awaits not the incoming breath, and so life ends." Death may be but a single breath away. Fail to take in the next breath, and immediately your afterlife begins. Each breath you exhale and inhale brushes shoulders with death. On December 31, one second after 23:59'59" it is 00:00'00". At the same instant, the thirty-first changes to the first, December gives way to January, and one year yields to the next. In the same way, this life transforms into the next life in the space of an instant. That is why the next life is contained in the "now" of this breath in and this breath out.

Therefore, the mind of darkness concerning the life after death should not be taken as ignorance of an event that is still half a century away. It is rather the mind of ignorance concerning now, this very moment—ignorance concerning *the present self.* The dark mind is precisely what conceals our present self from us. When the darkness is lifted and we see ourselves as we really are, the past and the future come into sharp focus. Shinran's words on the revelation of his true self at the beginning of this chapter proclaim this fact. This revelation is not a matter of conjecture or imagination. It is a matter of direct experience.

THERE ARE NO "GOOD PEOPLE"

Nowhere in *Teaching, Practice, Faith, Enlightenment* or in any other of his writings did Shinran ever divide people into good and bad. In his view, all humans alike are evil, "foolish beings constantly submerged and constantly wandering for all these countless aeons, without ever a chance for liberation." That assessment of the human condition is unvarying.

There is a certain appeal in assuming that the category of those who are "evil" must refer to remorseless murderers or the like, but Shinran's sense of evil is far more inclusive. No such simplistic definition is possible. For Shinran, to whom it was revealed that all beings are evil, "evil person" was simply another way of saying "human being." This understanding has nothing whatever to do with traditional explanations of evil based on common sense, the law, ethics, or morality.

Then what did the words "good person" mean to Shinran? Naturally, they meant something different to him from the general notion of what passes for a good person. Nor does he refer to superhuman beings inhabiting some loftier plane of existence. Rather, a "good person" in Shinran's sense is one who congratulates himself on his own goodness: lost in unbroken darkness of mind, blind to his own true nature that renders him incapable of anything but evil, such a person is under the *illusion* that he is good. This category includes people who imagine they can do good

whenever they so choose; people who see good and evil in relative terms
("at least I'm not as bad as what's-his-name"); people who believe themselves capable of feeling at least some penitence toward others, or of feeling shame in the depths of their heart; and so on. These are the people
whom Shinran calls, in an ironic sense, "good."

He left no doubt of his meaning when he wrote this:

> The sea of all sentient beings, from time immemorial until
> this very day and hour, is polluted with evil and lacking in a
> mind of purity; it is false and deceitful, lacking in a mind of
> truth.[125]

To rephrase, the human heart, from ages past till now, is stained with
wickedness and lacking in purity; it contains nothing but falsehoods and
drivel, and not an ounce of truth.

Of course, every person who ever has lived or who will live is included
in the "sea of all sentient beings." How could Shinran speak with such
assurance about the entire human race? Because in the deepest sense,
one person is all people: the one is the all. The truth revealed to one individual is the truth of all, and the ultimate reality experienced by one is
the ultimate reality that all will experience. Shinran perceived in his individual truth the truth of all humanity, and he proclaimed the truth of
all in light of the truth of his own experience.

CHAPTER **20**

The Path to Rebirth in Paradise

As we saw in Chapter 11, Shinran taught that when darkness of mind is eliminated and the purpose of life fulfilled, two things become apparent simultaneously: one is the revelation of one's true self, and the other is the revelation of the truth of Amida's Vow. We have examined the nature of the former already. Now let us explore the meaning of the latter through the words of Shinran as recorded by one of his closest disciples in a book called *Lamenting the Deviations*. Here is the opening of Section Two:

> Each of you must have come seeking me, crossing the borders
> of more than ten provinces at the risk of your life, with one
> thing only in mind: to ask the path to rebirth in Paradise.[126]

After twenty years of preaching in the Kanto region, Shinran returned to his native Kyoto when he was in his early sixties. In the wake of his departure, a number of events and issues arose in the Kanto region to shake the faith of those who had embraced Shinran's teachings there.

Could there be any shortcut to salvation? Were they being led astray? What was the truth? Racked with uncertainty, people of Kanto set off to see the holy man in Kyoto, pinning all their hopes on him. The round trip meant a journey of sixty days on foot. Those who went had to cross over Mount Hakone, ford the Oi River, and navigate other danger spots, with murderous thieves and bandits lurking everywhere. Each one who made the trip did so literally "at the risk of [his] life."

No sooner did Shinran face them than he said plainly that they could only have come "to ask the path to rebirth in Paradise"—*ojo gokuraku*, literally to "go [and be] reborn [as a buddha in] Paradise." It is evident that Shinran's teaching consisted of nothing but the way to go to Paradise (the Pure Land), reborn as a buddha.

What is the "path to rebirth in Paradise"? It is Amida's Vow.

As we have seen many times already, Amida vowed to eliminate the mind of darkness and fulfill the purpose of life for all people. In other words, he resolved to dispel the darkness of uncertainty about what happens after death, and provide one and all with the vast security and complete fulfillment of knowing for certain that they will go to the Pure Land. Shinran accordingly taught that Amida's Vow is the path to rebirth in Paradise.

Those in Kanto whose faith in Amida's Vow had been shaken set off for Kyoto at the risk of their lives, driven solely by the intensity of their need to attain the complete fulfillment of knowing they would be able to go to the Pure Land without fail.

TRUSTWORTHINESS PROVEN

As a man was walking down the street, and was passing by the open window of a nearby house, he happened to overhear the people inside gossiping about him. "The trouble with him is he's got a short fuse and he's prone to violence," said one. "Oh, my!" said another. The man burst into the house and yelled, "What do you mean, I have a short fuse and I'm violent! Says who?" Then he proceeded to whack everybody there on the head. That settled the matter; everyone in the room saw that he lived fully up to his reputation.

When a friend repays the money you lent him is the moment when any doubts you may have had about his promise are removed, and you know he's as good as his word. In the same way, the moment you are granted complete fulfillment by Amida is when all doubt about Amida's Vow is swept away.

This is the meaning of the revelation of the truth of the Vow that Amida made to provide salvation into absolute happiness in this world and beyond.

> How genuine, the true words of Amida that embrace us and never forsake us, the truth that is absolute and peerless![127]

The cry "How genuine … !" is Shinran's expression of the revelation of the truth of Amida's Vow. It demonstrates his ringing belief in Amida's Vow, beyond the tiniest shadow of doubt. The "true words of Amida that embrace us and never forsake us," and the "truth that is absolute and peerless" both refer to Amida's Vow.

The complete fulfillment of knowing he would, without fail, be reborn in the Pure Land was Shinran's ultimate source of vitality to the end of his nine decades of life.

SALVATION OCCURS TWICE

Shinran's certainty of being reborn in the Pure Land can also be seen in the following quotation, the content of which is nothing short of amazing:

> I know in truth. The great bodhisattva Miroku has attained the diamond faith of enlightenment, the highest spiritual stage possible for a bodhisattva, and will indeed enter into supreme enlightenment beneath the dragon-flower tree at the dawn of the three assemblies. As all those saved by Amida have attained the diamond faith bestowed by him, at the moment of death each one will be reborn in the Pure Land of Amida and become a buddha.[128]

This means, "It is true! I, Shinran, am now on a par with the great bodhisattva Miroku, Buddha of the future. This is due solely to the wondrous power of Amida's Vow. Not only that, while Miroku will be unable to attain buddhahood for 5.67 billion years to come, I, Shinran, will attain it even as this life ends. Could any happiness be greater than this?"

Miroku ("Maitreya" in Sanskrit) is the bodhisattva at the highest spiritual stage but one, just short of buddhahood. Now that he is level with Miroku, Shinran experiences a joy in having been born human that will live within him, unchanged, till he dies. The words "I know in truth" are a shout of wonder at the clarity of his revelation. In effect, he cries, "Now I stand shoulder to shoulder with Miroku—and with my death I will even attain buddhahood before him!" Shinran is joyful, his mind swept clear of all doubt in the reality of Amida's salvation, which is conferred twice: once in this world and once again in the world to come.

The joy that Shinran felt at this moment is beyond ordinary imagining. Think of the excitement of someone winning a nationwide singing contest, or capturing an Olympic medal. To play down such happiness might seem surprising, yet how could it begin to compare with the happiness of having achieved the ultimate purpose of untold millions of lifetimes?

Many people even today are believers in Miroku, and to them these words of Shinran's must sound utterly foolish, like the ravings of a madman. It's not hard to see why, centuries ago, a famous scholar-priest on Mount Hiei in Kyoto declared *Teaching, Practice, Faith, Enlightenment* the work of a lunatic, and tossed it aside in disgust.

Shinran wrote often of the fact that Amida's salvation occurs once in this life and again in the next, and Rennyo also provided this clear explanation in question-and-answer format:

> Q: Are the salvation called *shojo*[129] and the salvation called *metsudo* to be understood as one benefit, or two?
> A: Those who are saved by Amida in a split second [*ichinen*] enter *shojoju*. This is salvation in this life. *Metsudo* means going to the Pure Land and attaining the same level of enlightenment as Amida Buddha. This is salvation after death. Accordingly, Amida's salvation must be understood to confer two benefits.[130]

The exchange may be paraphrased thus:

> Q: Does Amida's salvation occur once or twice?

THE PATH TO REBIRTH IN PARADISE   149

A : In this world we are saved to the same level as Miroku, and at the moment of death we attain supreme enlightenment in Amida's Pure Land. So Amida's salvation occurs twice.

ONLY AMIDA'S VOW IS TRUE

Now let us go back to Section Two of *Lamenting the Deviations.* Shinran's statement to the men from Kanto who had risked life and limb solely to hear from his lips the truth about the pathway to rebirth in Paradise was surely unexpected:

> Given that Amida's Primal Vow is true, the sermons of Śākyamuni Buddha cannot be empty words. Given that the Buddha's sermons are true, the commentaries of Shan-tao cannot be empty. If Shan-tao's commentaries are true, can the sayings of Honen be false? If Honen's sayings are true, how could what I, Shinran, say be false?[131]

Some may scratch their heads at this logic and wonder if Shinran did not have things backwards. Doubt had arisen in these men's minds as to the efficacy of Amida's Vow—did it really have power to dispel darkness of mind?—and they had just made an arduous journey solely to ascertain the truth; yet Shinran's explanation takes the truth of the Vow as its starting point. What is the meaning of this bold and paradoxical assertion, and what personal experience gave rise to it?

> In this world as fleeting and unstable as a burning house, inhabited by ordinary people beset by worldly passions, all is idleness and foolishness, utterly devoid of truth. Only the *nembutsu* is true.[132]

For Shinran, nothing was true apart from the Vow of Amida. In the quotation above, "Only the *nembutsu* is true" is simply another way of saying "Only Amida's Vow is true." Positive that nothing in this world could be relied upon except Amida's Vow, and grounded in a radiant and unswerving awareness of the Vow, Shinran was able to declare without hesitation that "Amida's Primal Vow is true." The truth of Amida's Vow formed at all times the starting-point of Shinran's philosophy.

CHAPTER 21

Knowledge of the World to Come

TRUE WISDOM

> Now I am drawing near the end of this life. It is absolutely
> certain: I will precede you to the Pure Land, and there I will
> surely, surely await your arrival.[133]

Here, Shinran was telling his followers, "I have come near the end of
this life. I will be sure to go to the Pure Land and await your coming.
See that you come, without fail."

When no one knows with any certainty what may happen from one
day to the next, how could Shinran speak with such apparent conviction? Let us examine another statement he made:

> Amida's unimpeded light is the sun of wisdom that destroys
> the mind of darkness.[134]

This means, "The light of Amida is the sun of wisdom that banishes
darkness of mind and clarifies where we will go after death."

Wisdom could be defined as the faculty of seeing ahead. In the worlds
of *go* and chess, the best players can see as many as twenty or thirty plays
ahead; the poorest cannot see beyond their noses, because they lack the
necessary wisdom. Who would not like to know the future? We all want

to live secure in the foreknowledge of what lies ahead. Uneasiness over the future is precisely what causes so many to turn to astrologers and fortune-tellers for clues.

A wise chess player is one skilled at winning, but what does it mean to be wise about life in general? This well-known passage by Rennyo gives the answer:

> Even if he knows eighty thousand teachings of the Buddha, a man who knows nothing of the life to come is a fool. Even a nun who cannot read or write is wise if she knows the life to come.[135]

Even if you have memorized the contents of all the sutras and books ever written, if you do not know what will happen after you die, you are a fool. If you do not know what will happen after you die, you are like a pilot flying without knowing where he is headed. Birth is the start of a life journey—what happens if the destination remains unknown? Here is a vivid description by a very successful salesman in Japan:

> "Where shall I go? Uh-oh, no clue what airport I'm supposed to land at. No map or compass, either, I see. Oh well, the fuel tank's full and the plane's in good shape, so I'll just sit back and relax. As long as I'm enjoying myself, everything will be fine—no need to worry about what lies ahead."
>
> In time, fuel starts running low. This corresponds to the waning years of life.
>
> "Oh no, I can't go on flying any more! I thought all would be well if I was enjoying myself, but this is awful. The terrain below is mountainous. Nothing like a landing strip in sight. What do I do! What do I do!"
>
> The pilot turns pale and panics, eventually crashing into the side of a mountain and bringing his life to its tragic end.[136]

Anyone who turns a blind eye to a future he cannot avoid deserves to be called a fool. The true sage is not one who knows many things, but one who knows the most important thing. Even if he cannot read or write, a wise person knows that when death comes—whenever that may be—he will go directly to the Pure Land. Rennyo tells us that the difference between the sage and the fool is the difference between having and not having this knowledge of the next world.

THE SUN OF AMIDA'S LIGHT

As Shinran wrote, Amida is praised by all the other buddhas and bodhisattvas as "Buddha of the Light of Wisdom," because he alone has power to destroy the darkness of mind—the ignorance concerning what happens after death—that is the source of human suffering.

> As only he can destroy the darkness of no light
> he is named the Buddha of the Light of Wisdom.
> All the buddhas and bodhisattvas
> together join in praising him.[137]

As mentioned above, Shinran called the light of Amida the "sun of wisdom." In ancient China it was written, "There are no two suns in the sky." In the same way, the light of Amida is the one sun that can destroy darkness of mind. The only way to become a person of wisdom who knows beyond doubt that he will go to the Pure Land is to have one's darkness of mind eradicated by the sun of wisdom.

"GOING IS EASY, AND YET FEW ARE THERE"

A common misunderstanding about Buddhism is that it teaches that when a person dies, he or she automatically goes to Paradise and becomes a buddha. Despite its prevalence, this notion represents neither the wider teachings of Buddhism nor any teaching of Shinran.

Only those who have experienced the immense joy and peace of mind of Amida's salvation can go to the Pure Land and become a buddha. Salvation becomes evident during this life and, at the same time, so does whether or not one will be reborn in the Pure Land. When darkness of mind is eliminated, in the space of time called *ichinen* (swifter than a nanosecond), the settled conviction arises that rebirth in the Pure Land is certain. This conviction bestowed by Amida is the sole cause of re-birth in the Pure Land.

It is something like the experience of a college applicant: until he learns he's been accepted, he's on pins and needles—but when a letter of accep-tance comes in the mail he rejoices, his mind instantly at ease.

Yet, despite what many people may think, not everyone can achieve rebirth in the Pure Land. Śākyamuni said, "Going [to Paradise] is easy, and yet few are there."[138] This is certainly a strange concept. If being re-born in Paradise is easy, then one would expect the place to be well pop-ulated; if hardly anyone is there, then how could going there be easy? What did Śākyamuni mean?

"Going is easy" refers to those who cross the sea of life's suffering on the ship of Amida's Vow of great mercy. For them, life is a pleasurable sea voyage on the way to the Pure Land. Traveling overland by foot is arduous, as one goes over high mountains and through deep valleys, but a sea voyage is carefree, with all the work left up to the captain. Once we board the great ship of Amida's Vow, the wind of his mercy carries us in comfort to the Pure Land; what could be easier?

Then why are there so few people in the Pure Land? Here is Shinran's explanation:

> Concerning "Going is easy, and yet few are there": "Going is easy" means it is easy to go. If we ride on the power of the Pri-mal Vow, we are sure to be reborn in the true Pure Land of Amida, so it is easy to go. "Few are there" means hardly any-one is there. Because so few people have true faith, rebirth in the true Pure Land is rare.[139]

This may be rephrased as follows: When Śākyamuni said it is "easy to go" to the Pure Land of Amida, he was referring to those already in the ship of Amida's compassion. Since Amida himself does all the work of transporting them, it is easier than words can say for them to go. The reason he said "few are there" is because hardly anyone boards the ship of Amida's compassion.

Rennyo's commentary is similar.

> The Great Sutra contains the words, "Going is easy, and yet few are there." This means, "If you believe in Amida alone, receiving the mind of vast security, it is easy to go to the Pure Land; but few receive this mind of faith, and so although it is easy to go, hardly any do."[140]

Here, "receiving the mind of vast security" and "receiv[ing] the mind of faith" both refer to being saved by Amida and settled in the ship of his great mercy, so the commentary could be paraphrased this way: "When you are saved by Amida and board the Vow-ship of his great mercy, it is easy to go to the Pure Land. However, few people actually board the ship, which is why Śākyamuni said, 'Going is easy, and yet few are there.'"

From aeons past, the ship of Amida's mercy has been anchored right before our eyes. The captain has been calling to us in a resounding voice, but even as we flounder, drowning, we are so intent on seeking logs and planks to cling to that we neither see the boat nor hear the captain's voice at all.

ONLY THOSE SAVED BY AMIDA

Shinran's writings give great prominence to Amida's dual salvation, with emphasis on the salvation that occurs now. There is no effect without a cause. Without entering salvation in this life (cause), we cannot hope for salvation upon death (effect). If you cannot cross the little brook at your feet now, how will you manage to cross the great river ahead? Only those who are saved in this life can be reborn in the Pure Land.

The debate described in Chapter 10 fully clarified the true intention of Amida, who vowed to save all beings twice. Through *futaishitsu ojo*, or salvation by Amida in this life, we find salvation amid the sufferings of this life, and through *taishitsu ojo*, or salvation by Amida upon death, we are born into never-ending happiness. It was Shinran who corrected the error of his fellow disciple Zen'ebo, who believed that Amida's Vow had reference only to salvation after death, not in this life.

Whether one gains eternal happiness or undergoes many lifetimes of further suffering is determined in this life.

CHAPTER 22

A World Where Mind and Words Fail

UNNAMABLE, INEXPLICABLE, INCONCEIVABLE BLESSING

When we are saved by the wondrous power of Amida's Vow, and our darkness of mind is eliminated, two things become clear: "Beyond any shadow of doubt, it has been revealed to me that I will go to Hell for all eternity" (Revelation of the true self) and "Beyond any shadow of doubt, it has been revealed to me that I will go to Paradise for all eternity" (Revelation of the truth of the Vow of Amida). Since both of these become clear simultaneously and remain so until death, they are known as the "unified twofold revelation of the self and the Vow of Amida," or simply, "twofold revelation."

How could anyone know at one and the same time that he was destined for Hell and for Paradise? A Japanese philosopher has introduced the concept of "absolutely contradictory self-identity"[141]; indeed, the world of twofold revelation defies common-sense explanation, and can only be described as a marvel. Shinran's writings are consistent in their praise of the wonder of twofold revelation. Here are two examples out of many:

> Of the five wonders, taught Śākyamuni,
> none is greater than the wonder of Buddhism.
> By "the wonder of Buddhism" he meant only this:
> the wonder of Amida's salvation.[142]

If anyone in this evil, corrupt world
has faith in the Vow of Amida,
unnamable, inexplicable, inconceivable
blessing fills his being.[143]

In other words, "How marvelous! Why should someone as evil as I am
be saved? Why am I so happy? So blessed? Why is my life preserved? It
is beyond all comprehension. Everyone who enters the wondrous world
of Amida's salvation is filled to overflowing with fulfillment and joy."

The lines seem to pulsate with the tremulous excitement Shinran feels
as he contemplates "unnamable, inexplicable, inconceivable" joy.

NONE IS TURNED AWAY FROM THE GREAT SEA OF FAITH

Before Amida's Vow, which fully provides
the means to save one and all,
mind and words utterly fail:
let everyone encounter its wonders.[144]

One is struck by the sense of helpless frustration in the lines, as if Shinran
were struggling to explain the flavor of a great delicacy to those who
have never tried it. His passion is unmistakable as he strives to convey
something of the powerful joy of salvation that fills his being. Elsewhere
he made the ringing declaration that this world beyond the power of
imagination or words to encompass is a "great sea of faith."

When I think of the great sea of faith, I see there is nothing to
choose between high and low or priest and lay, no distinction
between man and woman or old and young, no question of
greater sins or lesser, no debate over the length or brevity of
ascetic practice.[145]

In other words, Amida's absolute salvation is for one and for all, without
any form of discrimination. It is a world of complete freedom and open-
ness. After this strong opening, Shinran goes on to repeat the word *arazu*
("not") fourteen times to underscore his utter rejection of all human

knowledge. This is as close as he could possibly come to expressing the state of twofold revelation, that surpasses language and imagination:

> It is neither discipline nor goodness, nor sudden nor gradual, nor settled nor scattered, nor right visualization nor wrong visualization, nor awareness nor unawareness, nor lifetime nor deathbed, nor many invocations nor single invocation. It is only inconceivable, unnamable, inexplicable faith.[146]

There is an old joke that centers on the inadequacy of words to convey experience. An apprentice priest carrying a tray of live coals tripped, causing embers to land on his bare feet. Amused to see the boy hopping around, yelling, "Ow, it's hot!" the ill-natured chief priest of the temple ordered him to define the precise meaning of "it's hot." "Yes, sir," gasped the apprentice, but he was unable to come up with any definition. The chief priest berated him: "If you cannot explain something so simple, you will never become chief priest like me." Suddenly, at his wits' end, the boy flung the remainder of the coals at the old priest's bald head. The old man howled. "Agh, it's hot! What did you do that for, you idiot!" The boy retorted, "Sir, explain to me the meaning of 'Agh, it's hot!' If you cannot lecture on something so simple, you don't deserve to be head priest."

As this story shows, the most ordinary experience can be impossible to convey in words. Shinran attempted to convey the essence of the "great sea of faith" even though it cannot be expressed in speech or writing, or conceived of by the human mind. In the end, all he could do to express it was to speak of "inconceivable, unnamable, inexplicable faith."

It is easy to picture this holy saint with his hands pressed together in thanksgiving, tears of joy running down his cheeks.

FOR THOSE WITH NO CHANCE OF HAPPINESS, PERFECT BLISS

Kakunyo described the miracle of salvation in these words:

> The wondrous power of the Primal Vow caused to be born those who could never be born. That is why it is called the

"supreme vow of mercy," and also why it is known as "the straight way of Amida's salvation."[147]

In other words, "Amida's Vow has granted perfect bliss to one with absolutely no chance for happiness. I can only contemplate the Vow in deepest wonder." The Vow is "supreme" because throughout the ages, it remains beyond comprehension or imagination; the expression "straight way" is used because the Vow has power to save into complete happiness in the twinkling of an eye (*ichinen*, the smallest possible unit of time) and there can be no salvation faster than this.

What is the wonder of this Vow that causes to be born those who can never be born? Suppose there was a doctor who could safely deliver breech babies that all other doctors had given up on as undeliverable; surely the world's obstetricians would laud his achievement as a wonder of wonders.

In the passage above, "those who could never be born" means those having absolutely no chance of happiness. Those who were thrown into the depths of hopelessness as "never [to] be born" were in fact already "caused to be born" or granted perfect bliss. It is crystal clear that their birth did not take place after death. How great the wondrous power of Amida's Vow, precisely because it saves those trapped in despair with no chance of rescue! Amida's Vow transcends our powers of understanding. All we can do is praise it.

"Is there really any such world?" many may ask in wide-eyed wonder. Others will be more dismissive, refusing even to give the idea a moment's serious consideration. Shinran gently reminds such doubters, "When not even the bodhisattva Miroku, who is closest to Buddha, can comprehend the wonders of Amida's perfect, peerless wisdom, how can ordinary, foolish humans hope to understand?"[148]

CHAPTER 23

The Changes That Are Brought by Salvation

EVEN AFTER SALVATION, WE ARE NOTHING BUT WORLDLY
PASSIONS, YET THE MIND IS FREE AND HAPPY

Life has a definite purpose: to have one's darkness of mind dispelled,
and so achieve never-ending happiness. This is Shinran's crystal-clear
explanation. When one's darkness of mind is dispelled, what exactly
changes, and how? Let us again hear what Shinran has to say.

> Although darkness of mind already is dispelled, the clouds
> and fog of desire and lust, anger and hatred continually cover
> the sky of true and real faith. It is just as when clouds and fog
> shroud the sun-filled sky: Beneath the clouds and fog, all is
> light, and not darkness.[149]

In other words, when darkness of mind is dispelled, the naked self is revealed, made of passions such as jealousy and envy, and nothing else.
But however thick the layer of clouds and fog that covers the sky, as long
as the sun is shining, underneath the clouds and fog all will be light; in
the same way, although one does remain filled with desire, anger, envy,
and other passions, once darkness of mind is dispelled, the mind is free
and happy, as if at play in the Pure Land.

    In Buddhist teaching, desire, anger, jealousy, envy, and the like are
known as "blind passions." The human being is an aggregate of 108

blind passions; we humans are made of these passions, and nothing else.

In the passage above, all of the blind passions that constitute us are likened by Shinran to clouds and fog, and the world of Amida's salvation ("true and real faith") is likened to the sunny sky. When darkness of mind is dispelled by the sun of wisdom, one sees clearly that one's true self is composed of nothing but blind passions. Shinran's statement that "the clouds and fog of desire and lust, anger and hatred continually cover the sky of true and real faith" is a confession of the revelation of his true self.

Elsewhere, giving a similar depiction of the true nature of the self, Shinran declared that all humans are "overflowing … with passions, full of desire, our minds cauldrons of anger and envy," and adding that for as long as we live, this condition "never stops, never vanishes, never comes to an end for even a moment."[150] In other words, we human beings are passion incarnate, without a particle free from desire, and we will never be rid of the blind passions in this life.

But the sun of wisdom can fill the mind with light, even though it remains shrouded with blind passions, and make it as happy as if at play in the Pure Land—just as sunlight is able to dispel the darkness beneath clouds that obscure the sky.

If not for the sun, there would be no way to know of the clouds and fog covering the sky, nor would darkness itself be perceived as such. Neither would there be any way to know about a world in which, below the clouds, it is light and not dark. In the same way, until the sun of Amida's wisdom dispels our dark mind, we can never be aware that our true self is made up of blind passions, nor can we perceive the darkness of our own dark mind. Nor, of course, can we understand that the mind filled with pain and distress (blind passions) turns into a mind filled with joy, as if at play in the Pure Land.

Shinran's analogy deftly points out that the fulfillment of our purpose of life hinges not on the passions, but rather on whether or not our darkness of mind has been dispelled.

AN ASTONISHING HAPPINESS

Hearing the word "salvation," most people cannot help thinking that it must mean some sort of change in our mental state—that we become dauntlessly positive thinkers, or are able to endure suffering with a bit more grace, or some such thing. One writer has surmised as follows:

> Then, what changes? Possibly it is that even though we go on suffering, we are able to bear it. I am inconclusive on the matter because I believe that sometimes even those who have gained real faith can lose the strength to live. That has to be accepted as something "not in one's own discretion." [151]

Others apparently think that it means we are liberated from egotism, and become indifferent to the lure of money and things, living aloof to the temptations of the world.

The Chinese sage Lao-tse declared that happiness consists in "knowing sufficiency." In Japan, a book called *Seihin no shiso* [The Philosophy of Honest Poverty] became a bestseller after the market crash based on the bursting of the land-price bubble. Many people believe that the only way to be happy is to suppress desire; some indeed believe that unless all desire is rooted out, happiness can never be achieved. But in his debate with Socrates, Callicles mocked such people, saying that those who want nothing cannot truly be said to be happy, "for then stones and dead men would be the happiest of all." [152]

If we spend our lives attempting to satisfy our limitless appetites, we can never succeed, and we are doomed to suffer throughout our lives. No philosophy or way of thinking can show us the way out of this dilemma. Only Shinran pointed to the existence of an astonishing sort of happiness that we can experience without reducing or eliminating our besetting passions, likening it to the brightness of a cloudy day: "Beneath the clouds and fog, all is light, and not darkness."

This analogy represents another effort by Shinran to do the impossible—use words to portray a world beyond words or imagination. Words cannot express true salvation (twofold revelation), but since there are no other means of communication, he took on this impossible task.

SUFFERING TURNS TO JOY

His darkness of mind dispelled, Shinran is made to see himself as a passion-ridden being and declares in contrition, "How shameful, how grievous!" Simultaneously, his contrition transforms into joy. In an access of ecstasy, he shouts, "How joyful I am! ... My delight grows ever fuller." In this way, suffering is transformed to joy without any change in quality or quantity. To explain this wondrous reality, Shinran uses the following analogy.

> Hindrances of sin become the substance of merit.
> It is just as with ice and water:
> The greater the ice, the greater the water.
> The greater the hindrance, the greater the virtue.[153]

A great block of ice melts to form a great amount of water. In the same way, when darkness of mind is dispelled, the greater the intensity of one's desire, anger, and other blind passions, and the greater the joy of salvation. The very Shinran who is the vilest and most depraved of sinners is indeed the happiest and most blessed being alive.

Just as a bitter persimmon turns sweet, so a plenitude of blind passions (suffering) becomes a plenitude of virtue (happiness). On this point Shinran is full of certainty.

At age thirty-five, Shinran was exiled to the frozen wastes of far-off Echigo Province (today's Niigata Prefecture) in a wave of persecution against Honen and his followers. He expressed his outrage in these words: "From emperor to retainer, they rebel against Buddha's teachings and trample justice, giving anger free rein and committing great sin."[154] And yet, he also had this to say: "Had my great teacher Honen not been sent away by authorities, how should I have gone into exile? Had I not gone into exile, how could I have hoped to convert the people of Echigo, who live in such a remote place? All this is owing to my teacher Honen."[155]

The greater his lamenting, the greater his rejoicing. Here we see a demonstration of the Buddhist truths *ten'aku jozen* ("unhappiness changes to happiness") and *bonno soku bodai* ("passions turn to joy"): suffering transforms into delight, without any change in quality or quantity. This is the wonder of the great sea of faith.

> The more deeply I come to know of Amida's immense compassion, the greater my gratitude to the teachers who led me.

My joy grows ever fuller, my debt weighs ever heavier …
Mindful solely of the depth of Amida's benevolence, I pay no
mind to others' derision.[156]

In other words, "I can only marvel at the joy of my salvation. I am overflowing with elation and thanksgiving. Awakened more than ever to the
depth of Amida's compassion, I am prepared to carry on no matter what
revilement I may suffer."

Derision, name-calling, oppression—the greater the trials that Shinran
suffers, the greater his corresponding joy and gratitude to Amida, to the
end of his vigorous ninety years of life.

"The waves of all woe are transformed [to joy]." The joy that Shinran
surely felt as he wrote these lines fairly radiates from the page.

CHAPTER **24**

Lamenting the Deviations
and the Purpose of Life

BEING HELD FAST AND NEVER FORSAKEN

Lamenting the Deviations,[157] the classic work that has conveyed Shinran's teachings to generations of readers, has eighteen short sections. Their essence is contained in Section One, which in turn is summed up in the opening mention of "being saved through the wonder of Amida's Vow." This is nothing but an expression of twofold revelation, which is the salvation of Amida.

Despite its widely admired literary qualities, to readers without a proper understanding of twofold revelation, the book could prove as dangerous as a razor in the hands of a child; that is why Rennyo went so far as to warn that not everybody should read it.

Let us examine the opening of Section One.

> "I am certain to achieve rebirth in Paradise, being saved through the wonder of Amida's Vow": When you believe this, a mind intent on saying the *nembutsu* arises within you and, in that instant, you receive the benefit of being held fast, never to be forsaken. You should know that Amida's Primal Vow does not discriminate between young and old or good and evil; the sole requirement is faith.[158]

The meaning of this passage is as follows: Amida's Vow is the pledge Amida made to confer the benefit of being "held fast, never forsaken"—

absolute happiness—on all beings, enabling them to be born, without fail, in the Pure Land. When one is brought to a knowledge of the truth of the Vow and the thought of saying the *nembutsu* arises within, one is "held fast, never to be forsaken," thus entering into absolute happiness. No distinction whatever is made between good people and bad, or any other category.

People read *Lamenting the Deviations* for a variety of reasons: because of its literary style, because it is a famous book, because they are interested in Shinran. However, the best reason we can think of for reading it is to enjoy the benefit of *sesshu fusha*, being "held fast, never to be forsaken," which the book teaches. This means gaining the absolute happiness of being caught up in a firm embrace and never let go.

Part of us lives in constant fear of abandonment. We fear losing our health, our children, a lover, friends, a job, wealth and possessions, fame and social status. Like people stepping warily on thin ice, we are in trepidation, afraid that whatever happiness we cling to will slip away. Pleasures are as fleeting as a dream, we know, and such happiness as we lay claim to is a phantom thing, a will-o'-the-wisp. Time may be on our side for now, but the day is not far when we will be stripped of all we have.

Let us hear again what Rennyo has to say on this.

> At the moment of death, nothing one has previously relied on, whether wife and child or money and treasure, will accompany one. At the end of the mountain road of death, one must cross the river all alone.[159]

To rephrase, nothing one has depended on in life, neither family, nor money, nor things, is of any help when it comes time to die. Abandoned by all, one must depart this world alone. Stripped naked, where is one to go?

Many people have an image of a happy death as being one surrounded by a beloved spouse and many children and grandchildren, and indeed the support of family and friends can help us through the journey of life. But at the last moment, our hand drops from theirs and we are completely alone.

Just as the most beautiful blossoms must eventually fall, at the end of this life, whatever money and treasure we have struggled to amass, what-

ever honor or status may be ours, will all fall away. Each of us must depart this earth alone. What could be sadder than this? Everyone on
earth is headed for this great tragedy. Shinran, however, made clear for
all humanity the existence of absolute happiness. Once we know the
happiness of being firmly embraced without fear of abandonment,
we feel a surge of joy in having been born human. In the words of
Śākyamuni Buddha, "To be born human is a rare blessing—a blessing
that is mine!" This radiant joy of being held fast and never forsaken is
what all people seek, and its attainment is indeed the purpose of life.

SALVATION OCCURS WHEN A MIND INTENT ON
SAYING THE *NEMBUTSU* ARISES WITHIN

Lamenting the Deviations has had many appreciative readers, but how
many of them have realized that the purpose of life is to receive the benefit of being held fast and never forsaken? Perhaps it is like someone walking in the mountains who cannot make out the shape of the mountain
he is on. For now, let us consider when one receives this benefit. The
answer lies in these words: "… a mind intent on saying the *nembutsu*
arises within you and, in that instant, you receive the benefit of being
held fast, never to be forsaken."

Once we are held fast by Amida, never to be forsaken, we cannot
refrain from reciting the *nembutsu*: "Namu Amida Butsu." What is the
nembutsu? It is an expression of gratitude, itself the gracious gift of
Amida.

One is not saved the moment he says the *nembutsu*, nor does saying it
confer salvation automatically. Rather, salvation comes before one ever
says the *nembutsu*, when a mind intent on saying "Namu Amida Butsu"
arises. Before the first syllable of "Namu Amida Butsu" has left one's
lips, at the moment one intends saying it, salvation occurs.

THE MIND INTENT ON SAYING THE *NEMBUTSU*
IS THE GIFT OF AMIDA

What then is the "mind intent on saying the *nembutsu*"? This question
is of paramount importance, since this mind alone is the key to whether

or not one will be "held fast, never to be forsaken," and thus fulfill the purpose of life.

The nature of this mind is expressed in the opening words of Section One of *Lamenting the Deviations*: "'I am certain to achieve rebirth in Paradise, being saved through the wonder of Amida's Vow': When you believe this …"

To believe that you are "certain to achieve rebirth in Paradise" is to attain a mind of light and certainty about the afterlife, which means having no doubt in the Vow of Amida that will cause you to be reborn, without fail, in the Pure Land. "Being saved through the wonder of Amida's Vow" means enjoying the benefit of being held fast, never to be forsaken, as the wonder of Amida's Vow is revealed to you.

The following expressions from the opening of *Lamenting the Deviations* all refer to the selfsame mind: "[believing that] I am certain to achieve rebirth in Paradise," "being saved through the wonder of Amida's Vow," "a mind intent on saying the *nembutsu*," and "the benefit of being held fast, never to be forsaken." The different phrasings might seem to indicate four different experiences or steps, yet they refer to one and the same mind, arising in a single moment. A semblance of sequence is inevitable simply because words cannot be written or spoken all at the same time.

Because this mind is the gift of Amida, the believer is said to "receive" or "be granted" the benefit of being held fast, never to be forsaken. The mind thus granted is *tariki* or "other-power" faith—faith bestowed by Amida.

OTHER-POWER FAITH IS ALL THAT MATTERS

Acquiring other-power faith means receiving this mind from Amida and gaining the benefit of being held fast and never forsaken. As Shinran says:

> The settling of faith refers to the moment when one is held fast by Amida. From that moment until actual rebirth in the Pure Land, one is at the level of true settlement.[160]

In other words, the gaining ("settling") of faith refers to the moment of being firmly embraced by Amida. From that moment until death, one is at the fifty-first level of enlightenment ("true settlement"), the certainty of one's rebirth in Paradise an established fact.

Elsewhere Shinran refers to the settling of faith as the "acquisition" or "determination" of faith.

"Faith" here has nothing whatever to do with the sort of faith that hinges on the answer to prayers for prosperity, health, or any other boon. The faith that Shinran is referring to is the twofold revelation granted by Amida. This twofold revelation is gained in the moment when "a mind intent on saying the *nembutsu* arises within you" and you know the happiness of being held fast, never to be forsaken, thus fulfilling the purpose of life. This is other-power faith.

Shinran's masterwork, *Teaching, Practice, Faith, Enlightenment*, speaks of nothing but this. Shinran stressed that the purpose of life is fulfilled once and for all only by other-power faith. Section One of *Lamenting the Deviations* explains it as follows: "… Amida's Primal Vow does not discriminate between young and old or good and evil; the sole requirement is faith." To be saved, it makes no difference whether one is old or young, male or female, a philanthropist or a murderer, brilliant or stupid. Other-power faith is all that matters. Shinran's teaching drives home this important point.

Shinran further explains that the *nembutsu* we say after being held fast, never to be forsaken, is uttered in gratitude from sheer joy at having achieved the purpose of life. Rennyo makes the same point:

> To be "held fast, never forsaken" means that one is saved by Amida and will never be cast aside. Such a person is said to have gained faith. The one who has gained faith repeats "Namu Amida Butsu" asleep or awake, standing or sitting; this *nembutsu* should be understood as an expression of gratitude for Amida's salvation.[161]

The message is clear: Those held fast by Amida cannot help saying the *nembutsu* in a joyous, irrepressible outpouring of gratitude for their salvation. Yet there is a great danger of misunderstanding. Based on a misreading of the opening words of *Lamenting the Deviations*, even some textbooks state, "Shinran taught that all who say the *nembutsu* can go to the Pure Land [be saved]." This erroneous interpretation has unfortunately gained great currency in Japan and is in fact very dangerous. Shinran did not teach that saying the *nembutsu* is the only requirement for salvation; he taught that salvation comes by faith alone, and that the *nembutsu* is spoken in an outpouring of gratitude for the happiness that is granted by Amida.

SALVATION OF THOSE WHOSE SINS WEIGH HEAVIEST

To an adult, a razor is an item of great use, but in the hands of a child it can become a deadly weapon. *Lamenting the Deviations* is filled with razor-sharp words, like these from the second half of Section One:

> The Vow of Amida exists to save sentient beings who are deeply stained with evil and inflamed with passions. Once one believes in the Primal Vow, no other good is needed since there can be no greater good than the *nembutsu*. Nor is there any need to fear evil, since no evil can block Amida's Primal Vow.[162]

Let us rephrase the passage: How is it possible for the worst sinner to attain supreme happiness? Because Amida's Vow exists precisely for the salvation of he whose sins are greatest. It follows that anyone saved by Amida's Vow has no need for any good, nor any fear of evil. Why? Because no greater happiness exists than Amida's salvation, and no evil is capable of destroying that happiness.

Shinran's teaching is often identified with the phrase *akunin shoki* ("the evil person is the true object of salvation"), specifying that Amida's Vow is for the salvation of evildoers, which we all are. On hearing this, one might not actually tell oneself, "Since evildoers are Amida's chosen guests, I'm done with good; might as well go out and commit more evil"—and yet many people must feel something like that. Without twofold revelation of the true nature of one's self and the truth of Amida's Vow, one is apt to come to great harm.

"CAN ONE AS EVIL AS I BE SAVED?"

If someone suffering from a terrible disease is cured by a sovereign remedy, why should he go off in search of any other medicine? Only a person not fully cured would have any need for another medicine. In the same way, the practitioner of the *nembutsu* who has definitely been saved has no possible need to engage in good works for the sake of his salvation. The very desire to do so is proof that one is not saved.

When you are filled with the joy of being "held fast, never to be forsaken," and thus achieve the purpose of life, the inestimable dignity of each passing moment of life is brought home with great power, and you cannot help devoting yourself utterly to expressions of deepest gratitude and attempts to make recompense (good works). Yet in so doing, there is not the slightest intent to do good *in order to* be saved by Amida. That is the meaning of the words, "No other good is needed, since there can be no greater good than the *nembutsu*."

One who is saved is awakened to the reality that he is a monstrous sinner, vile beyond compare (revelation of the true self), and amazed to find himself Amida's honored guest (revelation of the truth of Amida's Vow). Therefore the evil in his heart holds no terror for him. That is the meaning of the words, "Nor is there any need to fear evil, since no evil can block the Primal Vow of Amida." Only a person not yet revealed to himself as an unspeakable sinner without hope of salvation would wonder, "Can someone as evil as I really be saved?"

Shinran declared that a person of the *nembutsu*—one who has been saved, who has been revealed to himself as a vile sinner inflamed with passions and deeply stained with evil—lives in supreme contentment in a world transcending good and evil, neither aspiring to the one nor fearful of the other.

CHAPTER 25

The Path of No Hindrance

WHAT IS TRUE FREEDOM?

"No one is truly free, they are a slave to wealth, fortune, the law, or other people"; so the Greek playwright Euripides (ca. 480–406 BC) is said to have declared. The celebrated novelist Soseki Natsume opened his 1906 novel *Kusamakura* [Pillow of Grass] with these words: "Live by intellect, and you become rigid and inflexible; dip your oar in the stream of emotion, and you risk being swept away; cling to opinion, and you become narrow-minded. This world is hard to navigate."[163] French philosopher Jean-Jacques Rousseau (1712–78) observed in "The Social Contract," "Man was born free, and everywhere he is in chains."[164] People's laments over lack of freedom are always the same. East and West, in old times and new, children are hamstrung by their parents' expectations, fathers are tied to their jobs, wives are hemmed in by demands of home and family, old people live confined in small rooms. We long for freedom, yet we cannot find it.

Shinran, however, spoke of *muge no ichido*, or the "path of no hindrance." Section Seven of *Lamenting the Deviations* says this:

> Those of the *nembutsu* are on the path of no hindrance. Why is this so? Before practitioners of faith, gods of heaven and earth bow down in reverence, and evil spirits and heretics can pose no obstacle. Such people are unaffected by any recom-

pense for evil, and beyond the reach of every possible good; thus they are on the path of no hindrance.[165]

To paraphrase: "Those who are 'held fast, never to be forsaken' by Amida's compassion are in a wonderful world where no impediment poses any hindrance. Why? Because before practitioners who have received other-power faith, gods above and below bow their heads in reverence, and evil spirits and heretics are confounded. No recompense for evil bothers such people, nor can the efforts of even the finest individual yield any outcome equal to the absolute freedom they enjoy."

The first sentence is a surprising declaration: "Those of the *nembutsu* are on the path of no hindrance." The expression "those of the *nembutsu*" might appear to include any and all who intone "Namu Amida Butsu," but in fact, the heart of each one is different—just as tears, though unvarying in their scientific composition, may be shed out of sadness or frustration or joy. According to Shinran, people who say the *nembutsu* fall into three categories. First are those to whom saying the *nembutsu* is merely one good deed among many; second are those to whom it represents far and away the greatest good; and third are those so full of happiness at their salvation that they cannot help saying the *nembutsu* in an outpouring of joy. The passage above pertains to this last type. Having gained other-power faith and achieved the supreme happiness of being "held fast, never to be forsaken," these people of the *nembutsu* are truly "practitioners of faith," as the passage goes on to call them.

THE PATH ONCE HATED BECOMES A DELIGHT

How is it possible to enjoy perfect freedom in a world filled with constraints? It is difficult to explain in terms that everyone can understand, but perhaps the following story will give some idea.

A young boy took a path over a mountain every day on his way to and from school. On days when he stayed late for some after-school activity, the mountain would be scarily dark on his way home. In summer the sun burned fiercely hot, and in winter he was often forced to crouch down amid the howling winds of a blizzard. Rain turned the hilly path to a cataract. Filled with resentment, the boy would frequently mutter to himself, "If only the school were closer … if only this mountain weren't here …"

Then one day a pretty little girl transferred to his school. As it turned out, she was from his same village. The two of them began walking to and from school together, chatting about how far the way was and how deserted the mountain. In no time they were fast friends.

On their way home one afternoon, a sudden cloudburst hit them. The rain showed no sign of letting up. Between them they had only one umbrella, the little girl's. Finding himself cozily sharing an umbrella with her, the boy prayed silently all the way home: "Don't let the rain stop … let the mountain be more deserted … let the village be farther away …"

The things that had previously tormented him—the great length, difficulty, and isolation of the mountain path—had not changed, and yet they no longer gave him concern. Once obstacles to the boy's pleasure, they now became part and parcel of it. Everyone has probably had a similar experience at one time or another.

FREEDOM AMID CONSTRAINTS

Let us return to the passage above from *Lamenting the Deviations*.

It should not be inferred that because "gods of heaven and earth bow down in reverence" before the practitioner of faith, he or she is accorded universal respect; after all, Shinran himself was a constant target of slander and abuse. Rather, the statement means that gods of heaven and earth are awed by the wonder of Amida's Vow that destroys the mind of darkness, and by the believer's determination to spread word of the Vow.

Likewise, the phrase "evil spirits and heretics can pose no obstacle" does not mean that misfortune and calamity will disappear, or that there will be an end to the criticism and attacks of non-Buddhists and heretics. It means rather that once people know the joy of living, and rejoice in having been born human, then no matter what scorn or persecution they may experience, their conviction and progress are undeterred as they spread word of the wonders of Amida's Vow. "Mindful solely of the depth of Amida's benevolence, I pay no mind to others' derision."[166] Herein lies the secret of the mental toughness, rigor, and courage that enabled Shinran to keep pushing forward throughout his ninety years, alone and encircled by foes.

What does "unaffected by any recompense for evil" mean? It means that no return for evil has any effect on Amida's salvation—the great peace of mind that comes from knowing rebirth in the Pure Land is assured whenever death comes. The Vow of Amida was made for sinners destined beyond all doubt for Hell, capable of any vile deed. This is why a person of the *nembutsu*, or one saved by the Vow is "unaffected by any recompense for evil." Because he understands that no one can reap what he has not sown, through encounters with misfortune or calamity he is made deeply penitent for the evil that he himself sowed in the past. At the same time, he rejoices in the marvel of the power of Amida's Vow that has saved him, evildoer that he is.

Shinran himself, realizing he was a vile sinner, penned this heartfelt cry: "Pondering the Vow of Amida, I realize it was entirely for Shinran alone!" [167] All suffering is transformed in this way to penitence and joy, which is why Shinran declared that people of the *nembutsu* are "unaffected by any recompense for evil." These words from Section Seven of *Lamenting the Deviations* surely spring from Shinran's revelation that while he was "destined beyond all doubt for Hell," he was at the same time "destined beyond all doubt for Paradise."

Sadness and joy, anxiety and assurance, disaster and good fortune: all transform into the sheer radiance of life lived to the full. Because this is a world far surpassing all outcomes based on human effort, it is called the path of no hindrance, "beyond the reach of every possible good."

This, indeed, is the ultimate objective earnestly sought by all: finding the path of no hindrance, where in this life of constraint, perfect freedom may be savored.

CHAPTER 26

The Universal Purpose of Life

"Everybody has his own purpose in life. There cannot be one universal purpose for all."

Any follower of Shinran who hears such a claim will immediately be put in mind of a famous debate Shinran once stirred up when he was a disciple of Honen. He was opposed by three fellow disciples: Shoshinbo, Seikanbo, and Nembutsubo. Their disagreement is known today as the "Debate Over Sameness of Faith."

His three opponents argued as follows: "Our faith could not possibly be the same as Master Honen's faith. It has to be different. How could our faith be any match for his, when he is acclaimed as the most learned interpreter of Buddhism in all Japan?" Their deep respect for the master was evident, and yet Shinran attacked their premise straight on. "Master Honen's faith and mine are exactly the same," he declared. "That is not to say that I am his equal in wisdom, learning, or resources. I am speaking only of faith." This statement astonished and shocked the trio. In the end, they came to despise Shinran for showing what they saw as disrespect to the master; to them, he was a pompous ass who needed to be put firmly in his place. Evidently they could not conceive of faith existing apart from such human attributes as knowledge, learning, and experience.

Why bring up this debate here? Because, as we shall see, claiming that each person's faith is unique is exactly the same as claiming that each person has a unique purpose in life.

THE SAMENESS OF THE PURPOSE OF LIFE

The word "faith" may seem to people of no particular religious persuasion to have little or nothing to do with themselves; and yet if you think about it, there are many kinds of faith besides faith in a higher being. Without believing in something, we cannot go on, whether it be life and health that we put our faith in, or money and possessions, or honor and status. Children place their trust in their parents, husbands and wives in each other. To live, indeed, is to have faith.

Faith in tomorrow is the same as faith in life. If you believe you will stay vigorous, you have faith in your own health. Other things people have faith in include power and influence, science, medicine, and philosophy. The object and degree of such faith certainly varies according to the individual, depending on factors like intelligence, education, experience, and so on. The conclusion that faith is different for everyone seems inescapable. It is easy to confuse the various objects of people's devotion with the ultimate purpose of life, which would lead anyone to suppose that we all have a different purpose in life.

The opinion of Shinran's three fellow disciples could be paraphrased thus: "Master Honen's purpose in life is naturally different from ours. He is known far and wide as the greatest Buddhist scholar in all Japan; how could we, with our lesser learning and understanding, possibly achieve the same purpose in life as him?"

Shinran did not accept this way of thought, and was not afraid to say so. In effect, he told his fellow disciples, "The purpose of life is exactly the same for Master Honen and for me. That is not to say that he and I are on a par in knowledge, learning, experience, or anything else, but that the purpose of our having been born as humans is identical."

SELF-POWER FAITH IS NOT UNIVERSAL

Honen's word on the matter has been preserved. Referring to himself and Shinran by their earlier names, Genku and Zenshinbo, he had this to say:

Faith that varies is self-power faith; in other words, because each person has different knowledge, his faith is likewise different. But other-power faith is the gift of Amida Buddha bestowed on all men, good and evil alike, and so Genku's faith and Zenshinbo's faith are not a whit different. They are one and the same. I do not have faith because of my own cleverness. Anyone whose faith is different from mine cannot go to the Pure Land where I am going. Let there be no mistake.[168]

The clarity of the master's declaration is unequivocal. Those whose faith is different from his have only impermanent self-power faith, which is faith based on the shifting sands of knowledge, learning, experience, and the like.

The world is certainly unequal. People are clever or foolish, good or bad, tall or short, with no two the same; we are also infinitely various in terms of, for instance, our education, talents and abilities, and experience. Self-power faith, which is formed from convictions based on such variables, cannot possibly be the same for all.

Long ago, a man from a mountain village and a man from a fishing village, each on his way to see the city sights, stayed in the same lodgings one night and got into a quarrel. "Now you listen to me," said the first fellow. "I say the sun rises and sets in the mountains." "Don't be foolish," replied the second fellow, not giving an inch. "The sun rises and sets in the ocean. I ought to know, I see it every day." Along came the proprietor and laughed in their faces. "You're both wrong. The sun rises and sets among the rooftops!"

We each perceive things differently according to our own situation. To a wealthy individual, the ticking of the clock may sound like a reminder to put his money safely in the bank, while to someone in debt, it may serve as a reminder that time is running out. In the same way, self-power faith varies according to the individual experience and circumstances of each person; diversity is the distinctive feature of self-power faith.

In Honen's words, "Faith that varies is self-power faith; in other words, because each person has different knowledge, his faith is likewise different." In common usage, "faith" refers to self-power faith, and so the idea that faith is different for different people has gained wide currency; no one knows about or can begin to imagine a faith that is the same for one and all. By the same token, the assumption that there could never be a common purpose in life for everyone comes naturally. Those who pride themselves on their good sense are especially likely to conclude, "To each his own; all are different and all are valid."

A FAITH THAT IS TRULY UNIVERSAL

Yet Honen here proclaimed the real existence of a faith that is truly universal. He declared, "Other-power faith is the gift of Amida Buddha bestowed on all men, good and evil alike, and so my faith and Shinran's faith are not a whit different. They are one and the same."

"Other-power faith" is faith that all humanity can share in alike. It is freely bestowed by Amida Buddha without regard for intelligence or ability, learning or experience, morality or any other criteria. That is why to Honen there can be no differences in faith received through Amida's all-embracing compassion; Honen's faith and Shinran's are both other-power faith, and as such they are "not a whit different. They are one and the same." To use a modern analogy, if the TV station is the same, then the program received on every viewer's TV, whether large or small, old or new, must be the same as well.

That is why, in speaking of the rise of other-power faith, we use expressions like "obtain," "gain," "receive," and the like: this faith is a gift from Amida.

At the end of his statement, Honen makes it perfectly clear. In effect, he says, "My faith is other-power faith, which has nothing to do with wisdom, learning, or the like. Anyone who has self-power faith cannot go to the Pure Land where I am going. Make certain that you understand the difference between the two."

We see, then, that it is due entirely to faith received from Amida that the root of all suffering is cut off and we achieve the purpose of life, rejoicing that we were born human. Shinran, who had the courage to argue the unpopular side of this debate with his fellow disciples, and who thereby laid bare the nature of the world of other-power faith, also wrote as follows:

Layman, saint, villain,[169] slanderer,[170] saved alike by Amida,
Like all the drops gathered to the sea, becoming one in flavor.[171]

The water-drops in all the rivers flow into the sea and become one in flavor; the salty taste of the sea is everywhere the same. In the same way, those who obtain other-power faith (are "saved alike by Amida") all achieve the one purpose of life. They may be talented or untalented, able-bodied or disabled, rich or poor, of any race or occupation—it makes no difference whatever. All can share equally in the same world of joy.

Shinran could not have been clearer in showing that the purpose of life is indeed the same for all people everywhere.

CHAPTER 27

Knowing the Difference Between the Purpose and Means of Living

THE CONSUMMATE SWIFTNESS OF SALVATION

Shinran used the word *ichinen* in two different senses. One refers to the absolute happiness ("path of no hindrance") of attaining the purpose of life, as we have seen. The other means the smallest possible unit of time, with reference to the lightning swiftness of Amida's salvation. Shinran wrote that salvation is *gokusoku ennyu*, where *gokusoku* means "exceedingly swift" and *ennyu*, "perfect, without flaw." Salvation that required time to take effect could hardly be "exceedingly swift," and salvation that was unfinished could hardly be "perfect, without flaw."

In *Teaching, Practice, Faith, Enlightenment*, Shinran writes, "*Ichinen* indicates the utmost speed of the onset of faith."[172] By "the onset of faith" he refers to the fulfillment of life's purpose—the joyous moment when we realize, "*This* is why I was born human!"—and declares that it takes place with immeasurable swiftness or "utmost speed," in less than a nanosecond.

Why must Amida's salvation be so fast? Shinran's great-grandson Kakunyo explained it as follows:

> Amida's great compassion is aimed at saving one who is but a single moment from death. Were the Primal Vow to require several moments to take effect, how could one with but a moment of life remaining, the end nigh, ride on the Primal Vow?

That is why *ichinen* salvation is the vital linchpin and fountain-head of the true sect.[173]

To paraphrase: Amida's compassion is so thoroughgoing that its chief object is an individual in the worst-case situation of having only one moment left before dying. If salvation took longer than a moment, such a person could not be saved. Therefore *ichinen* salvation is indeed the main point of, and in it lies the distinctive character of, Amida's salvation.

In this way—calling it the "vital linchpin" and the "fountainhead"—Kakunyo emphasized in the strongest terms possible the supreme importance Shinran placed on *ichinen* salvation.

MIND'S DEATH AND MIND'S BIRTH

The consummate swiftness of *ichinen* salvation is expressed figuratively in this old Buddhist saying: "Light comes and darkness goes. Darkness goes and light comes." Which happens first? Does the light first come and the darkness then leave, or does the darkness first vanish and the light shine afterward? Neither statement is right, or rather both are—but human tongue and pen cannot comprehend the two simultaneously.

To address this dilemma, Shinran tried dividing *ichinen* into two parts, *zennen* ("former-moment") and *gonen* ("latter-moment"), to indicate the perishing of the believer's former life and the birth of Amida's life in him immediately thereafter. He wrote,

> Revelation of the Primal Vow means the end of life in the former-moment. Gaining immediate salvation means immediate birth in the latter-moment.[174]

In other words, when the truth of Amida's Vow is revealed to me, my life of illusion ends in the former-moment. Simultaneously, the life of Amida is born within me in the latter-moment, which is called "gaining immediate salvation." As the dark mind dies, the mind of light is born. Amida causes me to experience the death of this one mind and the birth of the other at precisely the same time.

The nature of the mind that vanishes can be expressed variously:

"What will happen when I die?"

"As I am, won't I go to Hell?"

"Everybody has his own purpose in life; there is no one, universal purpose."

"There's no such thing as absolute happiness."

"I don't know why I should go on living when life is so painful."

"I don't know why human life is of incalculable worth."

With the vanishing of this dark mind, full of anxiety over what lies beyond death and unsure of salvation, there arises the mind of light, certain of its destination in the afterlife and full of joy. The mind of light can be expressed through these words:

"Whatever happens to anyone else, I am certain to go to Paradise."

"I am content to live and content to die."

"*This* is why I was born human!"

"With every breath I take, I feel supremely contented."

"That *I* should have achieved this absolute happiness is a wonder of wonders."

"I am the happiest person in the universe!"

In this way, the worst possible situation is transformed to the best possible situation. An anonymous poet has expressed the experience metaphorically, using the petals of the lotus blossom, a kind of water lily:

When the petal falls
is when it floats—
lotus blossom

This and other analogies can capture only part of the experience of *ichinen* salvation, which remains in the end "unnamable, inexplicable, incomprehensible."

Kakunyo also wrote this about Amida's *ichinen* salvation: "The onset of the salvation of *ichinen* means the end, the final passing, of illusion."[175]

"The onset of the salvation of *ichinen*" refers to the moment when the mind of light and certainty about the afterlife is born. At that moment, the mind that has been the source of all illusion and suffering perishes;

that is why Kakunyo uses the expression "the end, the final passing, of illusion." At the very moment when *ichinen* salvation occurs, the mind of illusion dies completely.

Elsewhere, Kakunyo wrote another brilliant account of that critical moment, which may be paraphrased thus:

> Though the body remains alive, the delusion of self-power (mind of darkness) that is the source of all suffering is destroyed in the moment (*ichinen*) when Amida grants us diamond-like faith, and we believe and follow the words of Buddha taught faithfully by the masters. This alone is called "casting aside self-power and entering other-power" and "gaining immediate salvation."[176]

KNOWING THE DREAM TO BE A DREAM

In *Teaching, Practice, Faith, Enlightenment*, Shinran proclaimed that this mysterious moment of salvation is a watershed that divides the purpose of life (the "why") from the means of living (the "how"): "Not knowing what is true [*shin*] and what is provisional [*ke*] causes people to miss the great benefit of Amida's compassion."[177] This can be rephrased as, "Because people do not know the true purpose of life, they do not experience the joy in living that causes them to rejoice, 'How wonderful that I was born human!'"

"What is true" refers to the purpose of living, and "what is provisional" refers to human relationships, hobbies, goals, and other things that give pleasure in life—what we may call the means of living. Inability to distinguish between the two prevents people from gaining the great benefit of Amida's compassion. Only at the moment of salvation, when the mind of darkness dies and the mind of knowledge of the true and the provisional is born, can people separate them clearly.

Compare it to the experience of dreaming. A person might dream he was in a fire, say, running for his life. Cornered on a rooftop, he faces his imminent end, knowing there is no escape—only to wake up, drenched in sweat, and discover that it was all a dream. While dreaming, he cannot know he is dreaming, much less perceive the real world beyond the dream. The moment of awakening is when he becomes aware of dream and reality simultaneously.

Just as we can know a dream to be a dream only when it is over, so we can perceive the temporal or provisional as such only when we have encountered the true through the grace of Amida. Knowledge of the true and the provisional comes at the same time.

The purpose of life is revealed in the moment when our darkness of mind is eradicated and, blessed by the compassion of Amida, we know the great joy of being alive: "To be born human is a rare blessing—a blessing that is mine!" At the same time, it becomes clear that the various activities, goals, and other things that make life pleasurable have all been simply means for achieving that purpose.

Why should we go to extraordinary lengths to live—including undergoing organ transplant surgery when organs fail? Why is it that we should never commit suicide, no matter how much we may be suffering? Why is each human life of incalculable worth? All other philosophies of life fail to provide answers to such questions, for one reason only: They do not distinguish between the *purpose* of living and the *means* of living.

The Vow of Amida is indeed a sharp sword that severs in the briefest of moments the true from the provisional in life. Shinran, having had clearly revealed to him in that brief flash (*ichinen*) what was true—*why* we live, life's true purpose—and what was provisional—*how* we live, the means of living—steadfastly lived out the remainder of his natural life, full of profoundest gratitude for the great benefits of Amida's compassion.

CHAPTER 28

How Shinran Lived After Attaining the Purpose of Life

FROM AGE THIRTY-ONE HE BROKE WITH BUDDHIST TRADITION

Shinran's true image has been consistently kept under wraps, and his teachings are largely misunderstood. He is widely praised by a broad spectrum of pundits, from right-wing commentators to left-wing thinkers, regardless of political or religious affiliation, and yet followers of Shinran cannot help but wonder if he is properly understood at all. He is often depicted as a meek and gentle figure, but there was more to him than that. Though the master possessed great personal charm, his words and actions were strict and uncompromising.

Shinran's portrait shows the features of a man who had weathered many a storm, and his calligraphy is so sharp it might have been done with a razor; together, his portrait and handwriting offer a revealing picture of the man. Shinran's intensity and his uncompromising nature come across most conspicuously in his words and actions, but of these the world knows little.

At age thirty-one, Shinran deliberately made an unprecedented break with Buddhist tradition: he began to eat fish, and he took a wife. (For those in the priesthood, vegetarianism was the rule, and marriage was unthinkable, as priests were expected to remain celibate for life. This did not stop many from ignoring the prohibition in secret.) Shinran broke these ancient taboos in order to emphasize that Amida's salvation is freely available to all people, as they are.

This radical step did not fail to stir a storm of controversy. Shinran's response was characteristically blunt: "Those who are called great priests or famous priests of large temples are hateful to me." [178]

Though gentle by nature, when it came to distortions of true Buddhist teachings affecting the outcome of myriad lifetimes, Shinran was a force to be reckoned with. When he was a disciple of Honen, his firm adherence to principle led to a number of historic debates with his fellow disciples. As we have seen, he and Zen'ebo argued over whether salvation took place during this life or not, with Shinran adamant that it most certainly did. This, one of the three great debates that Shinran instigated, created such feelings of resentment among his fellow disciples that they accused him of brazenly going back on Honen's teachings and setting himself up as a rival authority. In the end, they drove him into isolation.

THE LITTLE-KNOWN REASON FOR HIS EXILE TO ECHIGO

That Shinran was exiled to Echigo at age thirty-five is well known, but few know the real reason why. The main reason was his insistence on the centrality of the Buddhist teaching of *ikko sennen muryoju butsu*—that one must leave aside all other buddhas, bodhisattvas, and gods, and turn only to Amida. (This teaching is indeed absolutely central to Buddhism: Śākyamuni Buddha himself said that delivering this teaching was the single purpose of his coming to earth.) Many in power at the time considered Japan "the land of the gods," and the rejection of these traditional deities was seen as a despicable heresy that would turn society upside down. Accordingly, the wrath of the highest authorities and those in league with them came down on Shinran. He was sentenced to death, and it was only at the intervention of the chief adviser to the emperor that the sentence was commuted to exile.

Shinran did not hesitate to lash out at the injustice of the authorities: "From emperor to retainer, they rebel against Buddha's teachings and trample justice, giving anger free rein and committing great sin." [179] With these scathing words he gave vent to his fury at the self-serving actions of Retired Emperor Gotoba and others that led to the banishment of his master, Honen, and the executions of his fellow disciples.

Out of petty jealousy, some of Honen's disciples were accused of having used Buddhist teaching as a pretext to enter the imperial compound and mingle with the women there while the retired emperor was away on a pilgrimage. The disciple Anrakubo faced his attackers fearlessly and responded with force: "All I am doing is living out the teachings of Buddha. It is not I who am unhappy now, but those of you who attack me. I have no doubt that you will suffer the torments of Hell for all eternity." Outraged, Gotoba ordered Anrakubo and three others summarily beheaded on the riverbank.

Shinran declared Anrakubo's anger justified. The charges were patently false; but even supposing they had been true, those who leveled them were no less guilty, as the custom of pressing young girls into service at court and forcing them to submit to the whims of the emperor and others was long established. Shinran gave no credence to the authority of such men over him—not even when they branded him a criminal and exiled him to the distant countryside.

In his later years, Shinran wrote, "No one must ever think of using the power of authorities to spread the *nembutsu*."[180] In other words, he forbade his followers ever to spread Buddhist teachings under the banner of officialdom. His aversion for the authorities comes across strongly in his later correspondence; their true nature was clearly anathema to him.

After five years of harsh exile, Shinran moved east to Kanto, where his sworn enemy, the mountain monk Bennen, lay in wait for him several times beside a mountain path. Finally, having missed his chance there, Bennen forced his way into Shinran's dwelling. It is recorded in *The Biography* that Shinran "strode out to meet him, swerving neither right nor left."[181] His calm before the sword shows great courage.

Addressing Bennen, Shinran gently assured him that if he were Bennen, he would have set out to kill Shinran, too. He added that killing and being killed, hating and being hated, could alike be means of spreading the teachings of Buddha. Shinran's great and compassionate faith ended up bringing Amida's salvation to Bennen, who was radically transformed and changed his name to Myohobo.

"WHEN I DIE, THROW MY BODY IN THE RIVER"

Many people look up to Shinran, but few realize that he railed against heresy and false teaching, even condemning other Buddhist sects. Many believe that Shinran shunned all criticism of others' faith, when in fact he is the author of explicit denunciations such as this: "Ninety-five varieties [of religion] dirty the world; only the teaching of Buddhism is pure and true."[182] There are many similar declarations in *Teaching, Practice, Faith, Enlightenment*, including this one: "I vow to criticize heresies and false teachings."[183] However, they pass generally unremarked.

Shinran was equally unforgiving in his criticisms of other Buddhist sects and their leaders:

> But even those who have founded their own sect or faction disparage the true teachings of Buddha by claiming that Amida and his Pure Land are nothing but the human heart, and that to speak of them in any other sense is childish.[184]

He ends up savagely denouncing all the popular Buddhist leaders of the day—men like Saicho,[185] Kukai,[186] Dogen,[187] and Nichiren[188]—by lumping them together as "fellows who know nothing of true Buddhism." His scorn is relentless. In effect, he declaims, "Today's Buddhism has completely degenerated. There are plenty of temples and plenty of priests, but none of them knows the first thing about Buddhism. There are Confucianists aplenty, but they have no idea how to tell good from evil. Only the true sect of the Pure Land flourishes."

The gleaming rapier of Shinran's criticism extended even to fellow disciples of Honen who turned only toward Amida and devoted themselves to the *nembutsu*: "Because their darkness of mind is not dispelled, [even if they say the *nembutsu*,] they do not grasp diamond-like true faith."[189]

In his later years, to the band of seekers who traveled to Kyoto from Kanto, risking their lives to verify the path to salvation at his feet, Shinran asserted, "Though I may fall into Hell because of the *nembutsu*, I will have no regrets." After this staunch declaration of immovable faith, he turned away from them, saying, "Beyond this, whether to accept and believe in the *nembutsu* or reject it is entirely for each one of you to decide."[190] In effect, he was telling them, "Do as you damn well please!" The words have a combative air.

His stern devotion to truth never abated, even to the end of his life. He left these instructions to those around him: "After I die, throw my body in the Kamo River and feed it to the fishes."[191] The injunction sounds harsh and cold. And yet, by this deliberate flouting of convention, he was prodding others not to focus on trivial matters like the disposal of their material remains, but to quickly resolve their own spiritual darkness and attain life's purpose. To the end of his life, Shinran strove uncompromisingly to reveal the truth of Amida's Vow.

ALONE HE WAS BORN AND ALONE HE DIED

To the world, he was an object of scorn, a debauched priest who defiled himself by eating fish and taking a wife. To those in power, he was a criminal, fit only to be banished to distant Echigo. To his fellow disciples, he was an arrogant know-it-all who set himself up in rivalry to their beloved master. To Bennen, he was a sworn enemy, to be hunted down and assassinated. And yet, in the face of such opposition, Shinran boldly held his ground. He lashed back at his detractors, denouncing them as powers in defiance of the law, monks ignorant of the teachings of Buddha, Confucianists unable to tell good from evil, and people with dark minds "who do not grasp diamond-like true faith." His spirit strong, he declared, "The true sect of the Pure Land is now flourishing." One can only marvel at his sternness, his supreme confidence and his invincible bravery. Amida's great and marvelous power is called *tariki* or other-power; Shinran's vigor and determination in pushing forward alone reflect the strength of the other-power faith that he received from Amida Buddha.

Today, people are so busy that often they long to escape reality and enjoy a calm, easygoing lifestyle; to such people, Shinran's staunch, uncompromising nature may seem rather amazing for its sheer energy and force of will. In fact, it was precisely this uncompromising nature that brought him widespread revilement. He was called an enemy of Buddhism, a depraved monk, a devil, a madman; he was turned on by his fellows as a traitor and ingrate; he was banished into exile. And yet, for Shinran, Amida's Vow alone meant life, and working to spread the truth was his consuming passion.

The incident which best shows Shinran's insistence on protecting the integrity of Amida's Vow is his disowning of his son Zenran, which happened soon after a fire had burned Shinran's house to the ground.

On the twenty-ninth day of the fifth month of 1256, when he was eighty-four, Shinran disowned his fifty-year-old son Zenran, who was preaching false doctrine to the Kanto communities. Zenran would inform the faithful that he had been given a secret teaching by his father in the middle of the night, and then proceed to spread false doctrine. He was also praying to the old gods of Shinto, telling fortunes, and otherwise desecrating the true teachings. Shinran could not forgive such a violation of Buddhism by anyone, not even his own son. When Zenran remained deaf to his repeated admonishments, Shinran had no choice but to take the drastic and agonizing step of disowning him, which he did in a letter: "My grief knows no words, but from this day on I am no longer your parent, nor do I recognize you as my son. Nothing could sadden me more."[192]

These words of an agonized father are moving, but at the time they subjected Shinran to a new storm of name-calling and derision: "What kind of teaching is it that breaks up families? What kind of preacher cannot lead his own son to salvation? It's a joke that he wants to save others." This response was inevitable. Shinran must have been well aware that he would earn contempt for going so far as to disown his son.

In Shinran's final years, this single-mindedness and aversion to compromise never faded. To those who saw tolerance as the supreme virtue, such obduracy must have seemed beyond the pale. But had Shinran given tacit approval to his son's behavior, out of some misguided parental affection, how many untold billions would have missed the joy of true salvation? "Though my life were to end in myriad sufferings, never would I regret what I have done": The resoluteness of these words shows the moving spirit of self-surrender with which Shinran dedicated himself to guiding others toward attainment of the universal purpose of life.

Who has lived a life as lonely as that of Shinran? "Alone we are born and alone we die, alone we come and alone we depart"—his life and death perfectly exemplify this truth.

And so, in the winter of 1263, in Madenokoji-higashi, Kyoto, Shinran finally made the passage to the Pure Land. He was just completing his ninetieth year. Only four people attended his deathbed: his disciples Kenchi and Senshin, and his fifth and seventh children—a son, Masukata, and a daughter, the nun Kakushin. The simplicity of the scene was in full accord with the solitary devotion of the life he had led.

Gassho.[193]

Afterword

Why do we live? What is the purpose of life? Shinran's answer is unambiguous. "The purpose of life is neither to amass money and treasure, nor to win honors and status. It is to have the source of suffering eradicated and be filled with joy, rejoicing that you were born human, and live in never-ending bliss."

The purpose of life is also expressed as "enjoying the benefit of *sesshu fusha* (being held fast and never forsaken)," or as *muge no ichido* (the path of no hindrance). Delight in being alive radiates from the pages of Shinran's masterwork *Teaching, Practice, Faith, Enlightenment*, which begins and ends with the words, "How joyful I am!" It is a manifestation of the blazing joy of one who has attained the purpose of life.

"Why is it wrong to take another person's life?" When a child asks this question, too often adults are at a loss, unable to give a satisfying reply. For adults as for children, the greatest sadness is not to know the joy of living.

Humanity is befuddled, unsure whether life has any meaning, or why those in pain should bother to carry on. Amid this general confusion, Shinran's words ring out loud and clear: "How wonderful it is to be born a human being!" Once the essential dignity of human life is understood, people should see why organ transplantations to extend life are worthwhile, why suicide is never a good option, why every human life is infinitely precious. Then, with doubts over the meaning of human existence resolved, each one can go resolutely forward to work on whatever besetting problems there may be.

Once life's true purpose is known, all trouble and suffering acquires meaning. Live for life's true purpose, and all your efforts are sure to be rewarded.

NOTES

Part One: The Human Condition
1 The boy in question is one of the authors of this book, Kentaro Ito.

2 Fraser, *White-Collar Sweatshop*, 9–10.

3 Nietzsche, *On the Genealogy of Morals*, 136.

4 Rilke, "The Neighbor." The final verse of this short poem reads: Why must I always have as neighbor / him who makes you fearfully sing / and say that life is heavier / than the heaviness of all things?

5 Morotomi, *Munashisa no shinrigaku*, 4–5.

6 Frankl, *Man's Search for Meaning*, 112, 143.

7 "In Harm's Way." National Institute of Mental Health.

8 Brent, "Suicide in Youth." The Nation's Voice on Mental Illness.

9 "Attacks on Homeless Reported Nationwide." The Associated Press.

10 "CDC Reports Latest Data on Suicide Behaviors, Risk Factors, and Prevention."

11 Foot, "Moral Relativism," 34–35.

12 Durkheim, *Suicide*, 257.

13 Csikszentmihalyi, *Flow*.

14 Kentaro Ito.

15 Moskowitz, *In Therapy We Trust*, 255.

16 Russell, *The Conquest of Happiness*, 121.

17 "*Kin medarutte shiawase nanka ja nakatta*," 46.

18 Zeldin, *An Intimate History of Humanity*, 15.

19 Durkheim, *Suicide*, 248.

20 Pascal, *Pensées*, 61.

21 Leavy, "The Price of Fame," 56. Quoted from Jordan, *Rare Air*, 58.

22 Murakami, *Kaiten mokuba no deddo hiito,* 13.

23 Miller, *Death of a Salesman*, 10.

24 Alighieri, *The Divine Comedy*, 1.

25 Words and music by George David Weiss, Hugo Peretti, and Luigi Creatore.

26 Shakespeare, *Romeo and Juliet*, II. vi. 9–11.

27 Eto, "*Tsuma to watashi*," 119–26.

28 Hilty, *Kofukuron*, 14. (The quote is translated from the Japanese translation of

the German book, *Glück* [Happiness].)

29 Goethe, *The Sorrows of Young Werther*, 33.

30 Distel, *Renoir*, 121.

31 Words and music by John Lennon and Paul McCartney.

32 Alighieri, *The Divine Comedy*, 7.

33 Ohira, *Yasashisa no seishin byori*, 120–21.

34 Shakespeare, *King Lear*, I. iv. 280–81.

35 Plato, "Symposium," 164.

36 Goethe, *Faust*, 11.

37 Ninomiya, "*Onizuka Katsuya: Dokuhaku yojikan*," 185.

38 Kohn, *No Contest*, 111.

39 Ruben, *Competing*, 142.

40 Singer, *Meaning in Life*, 92.

41 Trump and Leerhsen, *Surviving at the Top*, 11.

42 Schopenhauer, *The World as Will and Representation*, 312.

43 Shakespeare, *Hamlet*, IV. iv. 53.

44 Busse, "Over the Mountains."

45 Kitagawa and Tsuchida, *The Tale of the Heike*, 5. The temple referred to is an Indian monastery built in honor of Śākyamuni Buddha.

46 Didion, *The Year of Magical Thinking*, 3.

47 Ibid., 6–10.

48 Kishimoto, *Shi o mitsumeru kokoro*, 132.

49 Sartre, *Being and Nothingness*, 784.

50 Nietzsche, *Thus Spake Zarathustra*, 189.

51 Miyadai, *Jiyu na shinseiki, fujiyu na anata*, 94.

52 Miyadai and Fujii, *Utsukushiki shonen no riyu naki jisatsu*, 40–41.

53 Ibid., 34.

54 Miyadai et al., *Shinseiki no riaru*, 58.

55 Camus, *The Myth of Sisyphus*, 26.

56 Tanaka, *Jinsei no mokuteki wa nan desu ka*, 35

57 Tillich, *The Courage to Be*, 39.

58 Shakespeare, *Measure for Measure*, III. i. 11. "Merely, thou art Death's fool. / For him thou labour'st by thy flight to shun / And yet runn'st toward him still."

59 "Chapter on the True Buddha and Land" in *Teaching, Practice, Faith, Enlightenment*.

Part Two: The Words of Shinran

[60] Einstein, *The World As I See It*, 1.

[61] *Kyogyoshinsho* (*Teaching, Practice, Faith, Enlightenment*) is Shinran's lifework, containing all of his teachings. After finishing a rough draft in his early fifties, he continued to refine it the rest of his life, editing and amending it.

[62] "Preface" in *Teaching, Practice, Faith, Enlightenment*.

[63] In James, *The Varieties of Religious Experience*, 137.

[64] Akutagawa, *Shuju no kotoba*, 30.

[65] "Chapter on Practice" in *Teaching, Practice, Faith, Enlightenment*.

[66] "Houses" refers to the six worlds of suffering. Buddhism teaches that just as a wheel keeps turning without end, so all beings travel endlessly back and forth among these six worlds in constant suffering.

[67] Dostoevsky, *Memoirs from the House of the Dead*, 24.

[68] Sung by Harumi Miyako, lyrics by Tetsuro Hoshino.

[69] From *Panegyric*, by Shinran's great-great-grandson Zonkaku (1290–1373).

[70] *Hymns on the Masters*.

[71] Honen's real name.

[72] *Hymns on the Masters*.

[73] Kishimoto, *Shi o mitsumeru kokoro*, 16–17.

[74] Tolstoy, "A Confession," 31.

[75] Pascal, *Pensées*, 51.

[76] Seneca, *"Kofuku na jinsei ni tsuite,"* 124–25.

[77] Chekhov, "Ward No. 6," 195.

[78] "Preface" in *Teaching, Practice, Faith, Enlightenment*.

[79] By Enomoto Kikaku (1661–1707).

[80] *Lamenting the Deviations*, Sec. 13.

[81] "Chapter on Practice" in *Teaching, Practice, Faith, Enlightenment*.

[82] "Preface," Ibid.

[83] "Chapter on Practice," Ibid.

[84] *Hymns on the Masters*.

[85] "Chapter on the Provisional Buddhas and Lands" in *Teaching, Practice, Faith, Enlightenment*.

[86] *Hymns on the Masters*.

[87] Kamei, "Shinran," 228.

[88] A name Shinran used from the time of his exile, meaning "foolish person"; often simply "Gutoku."

89 The teaching, practice, and enlightenment referred to here are the gifts of Amida.

90 "Preface" in *Teaching, Practice, Faith, Enlightenment*.

91 "Chapter on the Provisional Buddhas and Lands," Ibid.

92 Shan-tao (613–81) was the Chinese master of Pure Land thought who inspired Honen.

93 *Hymns on the Three Ages*.

94 Iijima, *Katsushika Hokusai den*, 67.

95 Kakunyo, *Notes on Oral Transmissions*, Sec. 14.

96 "Chapter on Practice" in *Teaching, Practice, Faith, Enlightenment*.

97 "Chapter on Faith," Ibid.

98 Ibid.

99 Ibid.

100 Cassirer, *An Essay on Man*, 1.

101 Kierkegaard, *The Sickness Unto Death*, 62–63.

102 Sung by Kiyoko Suizenji, lyrics by Tetsuro Hoshino.

103 The literal meaning of "Ishikawa," the thief's surname.

104 "Chapter on Faith" in *Teaching, Practice, Faith, Enlightenment*.

105 *Hymns on the Three Ages*.

106 "Chapter on Faith" in *Teaching, Practice, Faith, Enlightenment*.

107 Watson, *The Double Helix*, 35.

108 Rennyo, *The Letters*, 1:11.

109 By Kinokuniya Mataemon (years of birth and death unknown).

110 Emerson, "Fate," 416.

111 Jung, *The Undiscovered Self*, 94.

112 *Lamenting the Deviations*, Sec. 13.

113 See the poem on p. 131.

114 *Notes on "Essentials of Faith Alone."*

115 *Hymns of Lament and Reflection*.

116 Nāgārjuna, *Ta-chih-tu-lun*.

117 *Hymns of Lament and Reflection*.

118 "Chapter on Faith" in *Teaching, Practice, Faith, Enlightenment*.

119 Itsuki, *Jinsei no mokuteki*, 131.

120 *Hymns of Lament and Reflection*.

121 *Lamenting the Deviations*, Sec. 2.

122 *In Praise of the Sacred Name and the True Image*.

123 *Lamenting the Deviations*, Sec. 3.

124 "Chapter on Faith" in *Teaching, Practice, Faith, Enlightenment.*

125 Ibid.

126 *Lamenting the Deviations*, Sec. 2.

127 "Preface" in *Teaching, Practice, Faith, Enlightenment.*

128 "Chapter on Faith," Ibid.

129 *Shojo* and *shojoju* refer to salvation by Amida, in this life, to the penultimate stage of the fifty-two stages of enlightenment.

130 Rennyo, *The Letters*, 1:4.

131 *Lamenting the Deviations*, Sec. 2.

132 Ibid., Postscript.

133 *Lamp for the Latter Age*, 12.

134 "Preface" in *Teaching, Practice, Faith, Enlightenment.*

135 Rennyo, *The Letters*, 5:2.

136 Okushiro, *Kyogo seerusu no himitsu*, 102.

137 *Hymns on the Pure Land.*

138 The Larger Sutra of Infinite Life.

139 *In Praise of the Sacred Name and the True Image.*

140 Rennyo, *The Letters*, 2:7.

141 Kitaro Nishida (1870–1945).

142 *Hymns on the Masters.*

143 Ibid.

144 *Hymns on the Pure Land.*

145 "Chapter on Faith" in *Teaching, Practice, Faith, Enlightenment.*

146 Ibid.

147 Kakunyo, *Notes Rectifying Heresy*, Sec. 10.

148 *Lamp for the Latter Age*, 7.

149 "Chapter on Practice" in *Teaching, Practice, Faith, Enlightenment.*

150 *Concerning Single Invocation and Many Invocations.*

151 Itsuki, *Jinsei no mokuteki*, 148.

152 Plato, "Gorgias," 276.

153 *Hymns on the Masters.*

154 "Chapter on the Provisional Buddhas and Lands" in *Teaching, Practice, Faith, Enlightenment.*

155 Kakunyo, *The Biography.*

156 "Chapter on the Provisional Buddhas and Lands" in *Teaching, Practice, Faith,*

Enlightenment.

157 *Tannisho* (*Lamenting the Deviations*), well known as an outstanding literary classic, contains the words of Shinran as recorded by one of his closest disciples.

158 *Lamenting the Deviations*, Sec. 1.

159 Rennyo, *The Letters*, 1:11.

160 *Lamp for the Latter Age*, 13.

161 Rennyo, *The Letters*, 1:7.

162 *Lamenting the Deviations*, Sec. 1.

163 Natsume, *Kusamakura*, 5.

164 Rousseau, "The Social Contract," 45.

165 *Lamenting the Deviations*, Sec. 7.

166 "Chapter on the Provisional Buddhas and Lands" in *Teaching, Practice, Faith, Enlightenment.*

167 *Lamenting the Deviations*, Postscript.

168 Kakunyo, *The Biography.*

169 One who commits any of the five deadly sins: patricide, matricide, killing an arhat, destroying the harmony of the *sangha* or fraternity of monks, or shedding the blood of a Buddha.

170 One guilty of slandering true Buddhism, the gravest offense of all.

171 "Chapter on Practice" in *Teaching, Practice, Faith, Enlightenment.*

172 "Chapter on Faith," Ibid.

173 Kakunyo, *Notes on Oral Transmissions*, Sec. 21. "*Shinshu*" (literally, "true sect") is the name of the Pure Land Buddhist tradition founded by Shinran.

174 *Gutoku's Notes.*

175 Kakunyo, *Notes on Steadfast Holding*, Sec. 5.

176 Kakunyo, *Notes Rectifying Heresy*, Sec. 19.

177 "Chapter on the True Buddha and Land" in *Teaching, Practice, Faith, Enlightenment.*

178 *Hymns of Lament and Reflection.*

179 "Chapter on the Provisional Buddhas and Lands" in *Teaching, Practice, Faith, Enlightenment.*

180 *Collected Letters.*

181 Kakunyo, *The Biography.*

182 *Hymns on the Three Ages.* The expression "ninety-five varieties" was used by Śākyamuni Buddha to refer to all religions other than Buddhism.

183 "Chapter on the Provisional Buddhas and Lands" in *Teaching, Practice, Faith,*

Enlightenment.

184 "Chapter on Faith," Ibid.

185 Saicho (767–822) was the founder of the Tendai sect of Buddhism and of its headquarters, the monastery Enryakuji on Mount Hiei in Kyoto. He is also known as Dengyo Daishi.

186 Kukai (774–835) was the ascetic founder of the Shingon sect of Buddhism, and of the monastic center on Mount Koya in Wakayama for the practice of esoteric Buddhist meditation. He is also known as Kobo Daishi.

187 Dogen (1200–53) was the founder of the Soto sect of Zen Buddhism and of the Zen temple Eiheiji in Fukui.

188 Nichiren (1222–82) was the founder of the Nichiren sect, which emphasizes belief in the Lotus Sutra; a vocal opponent of Pure Land beliefs.

189 "Chapter on Faith" in *Teaching, Practice, Faith, Enlightenment.*

190 *Lamenting the Deviations*, Sec. 2.

191 Kakunyo, *Notes Rectifying Heresy*, Sec. 16.

192 Ishida and Chiba, *Shinshu shiryo shusei*, Vol. 1, 422.

193 To place the palms together in an expression of gratitude.

GLOSSARY

AMIDA

The Japanese pronunciation of the name of the buddha Amitābha [Infinite Light] or Amitāyus [Infinite Life]. (Throughout this book, we have opted to use the Japanese version of his name rather than the Sanskrit.) Amida is supreme among the innumerable buddhas in the cosmos, all of whom achieved buddhahood through his power. See also Primal Vow.

BIRTH-AND-DEATH CYCLE

The same as transmigration. Buddhism teaches that from ages past, each of us has been born and reborn countless times in a myriad of life forms. Just as a wheel keeps turning without end, so all beings travel endlessly back and forth among the various worlds of illusion, in constant suffering.

BLIND PASSION; WORLDLY PASSION *(BONNO)*

Lust, anger, jealousy, and other delusions of the heart that trouble and torment us. Buddhism teaches that the human being is an aggregate of 108 blind passions; we humans are made of these passions, and nothing else.

BODHISATTVA *(BOSATSU)*

One who is striving to attain the enlightenment of a buddha.

BUDDHA

One who has attained the highest level of enlightenment in the cosmos. Buddhism teaches that there are fifty-two levels of enlightenment, the highest of which is called the "enlightenment of a buddha." The only human being on this earth ever to achieve supreme enlightenment was Śākyamuni. Buddhism further teaches that the cosmos contains innumerable worlds similar to ours, with as many buddhas as there are grains of sand in the Ganges.

DARKNESS OF MIND; THE DARK MIND *(MUMYO NO YAMI)*
The mind of ignorance about what will happen after death. The ultimate source of suffering.

HONEN (1133–1212)
The founder of the Pure Land School of Buddhism (Jodo Shu), and Shinran's teacher. Known for his profound learning and saintliness, he was widely revered as Japan's premier Buddhist scholar.

ICHINEN
Shinran used the term in two different senses:
1) The absolute happiness of achieving the purpose of life by having one's rebirth in the Pure Land assured.
2) The smallest possible unit of time, indicating the lightning swiftness of Amida's salvation.

KAKUNYO (1270–1351)
Shinran's great-grandson. He faithfully transmitted the teachings of Shinran, authoring numerous books.

KE
The provisional; human relationships, pastimes, and temporal goals. Used in opposition to *shin*.

LAMENTING THE DEVIATIONS (TANNISHO)
A classic medieval text that has conveyed Shinran's teachings to many readers. Also an outstanding literary classic, it contains the words of Shinran as recorded by one of his closest disciples.

LAW OF KARMA
A universal truth woven through all Buddhist doctrine. Good actions bring about good results (happiness); conversely, if we do bad things, then bad results (unhappiness, disaster) occur. The law of karma dictates that everything that happens to us, good and bad alike, is determined by our own actions.

NEMBUTSU

An expression of gratitude for the salvation granted by Amida. Recitation of the words "Namu Amida Butsu."

OJO

Amida's salvation. Composed of characters meaning "to go" and "to be born." Shinran taught that the word has two meanings:

1) *futaishitsu ojo* (literally, "salvation without loss of the body"): being saved by Amida into absolute happiness in this life.

2) *taishitsu ojo* (literally, "salvation with loss of the body"): going to Amida's Pure Land at the moment of death and being reborn as a buddha.

OTHER POWER *(TARIKI)*

The power of Amida Buddha alone.

OTHER-POWER FAITH *(TARIKI NO SHINJIN)*

Completely unlike ordinary faith, the faith which Shinran taught is the gift of Amida Buddha, and so it is called "other-power faith." It is also known as "twofold revelation" and "true faith." Shinran preached nothing but other-power faith.

PATH OF NO HINDRANCE *(MUGE NO ICHIDO)*

Absolute happiness. The state of mind of one who has been saved by Amida.

PRIMAL VOW; AMIDA'S VOW *(HONGAN)*

Amida Buddha made forty-eight vows, of which the eighteenth is known as the Primal Vow. Addressing all humanity, he said: "Believe me, and I will save you into absolute happiness without fail." This is the most essential and important of the forty-eight vows, revealing Amida's true intention.

PURE LAND; PARADISE *(JODO; GOKURAKU)*

The pure world inhabited by Amida Buddha.

PURE LAND BUDDHISM

In contrast to Shodo Buddhism, where enlightenment is achieved through the practitioner's own efforts, Pure Land Buddhism teaches salvation by Amida Buddha: anyone who believes in Amida's Vow will be reborn in the Pure Land and become a buddha.

Śākyamuni's seminal teaching about Amida's Vow was accurately disseminated by seven priests in India, China, and Japan. First, two renowned priests from India, Nāgārjuna (ca. 150–250) and Vasubandhu (ca. 320–400), systematized the teachings of Pure Land Buddhism. Later, Buddhism spread to China, where the great priests T'an-luan (476–542), Tao-ch'o (562–645), and Shan-tao expanded the teachings of Pure Land Buddhism and clarified the nature of Amida's salvation. No independent sect of Pure Land Buddhism was established in China.

In Japan, the Tendai master Genshin (942–1017) sparked an explosive spread of the teachings of Pure Land Buddhism through his book *Ojo yoshu* (Essentials of Rebirth), which also had great impact on Chinese Buddhism. Later, Honen founded the Pure Land School, and people all across Japan sought Amida's salvation. Feeling threatened, members of rival sects colluded with those in power to clamp down on the Pure Land School. Four of Honen's disciples were sentenced to death, while Honen and Shinran were banished to remote areas.

After Honen's death, divisions among his disciples caused the Pure Land School to split into five sects, among them the Seizan branch of Zen'ebo and the Chinzei branch of Shokobo. In order to transmit Honen's teachings accurately, Shinran founded the True Pure Land School. Shinran stressed that this was no new sect, but only a means of spreading accurately the teachings of the seven renowned priests before him. The True Pure Land School stands as the greatest sect of Buddhism in Japan to this day.

RENNYO (1415–99)

A descendant of Shinran's who transmitted Shinran's teachings faithfully to a vast number of people all across Japan.

ŚĀKYAMUNI (ca. 560–480 BC)

The founder of Buddhism. "Śākya" was his family's clan name and "muni" means saint, so Śākyamuni means "saint of the Śākyas." His given name was Siddhārtha Gautama. He was born in the Nepalese state of Kapilavastu, the son of King Śuddhodana. At the age of twenty-nine he left home in search of absolute happiness. Following six years of spiritual discipline, he achieved supreme enlightenment at the age of thirty-five and became a Buddha. From then until his death at the age of eighty, he taught throughout India the supremacy and compassion of Amida.

SESSHU FUSHA

Literally "hold fast, never forsake." Those who are saved by Amida Buddha into absolute happiness will never be forsaken by him. This phrase expresses the boundless compassion of Amida.

SHAN-TAO (613–81)

A monk who was one of the most important figures in Pure Land Buddhism in China, he helped to develop the school's teachings. His commentary on the Sutra of Contemplation on the Buddha of Infinite Life corrected errors in contemporary Buddhism and clarified the truth. Shan-tao's influence on Pure Land Buddhism in Japan was incalculable; Honen wrote that his teachings "came only from Shan-tao."

SHIN

The true; life's true purpose. Used in opposition to *ke*.

SHINRAN (1173–1263)

Also known as Shinran Shonin or "Saint Shinran." Founder of Shin Buddhism or the True Pure Land School (Jodo Shinshu).

SHOJO; SHOJOJU

Salvation by Amida, in this life, to the fifty-first of the fifty-two stages of enlightenment.

SUTRAS

Sermons delivered by Śākyamuni during the forty-five years between his attainment of Buddhist enlightenment at thirty-five and his death at eighty, as recorded by his disciples.

TEACHING, PRACTICE, FAITH, ENLIGHTENMENT (KYOGYOSHINSHO)

Shinran's lifework, containing all of his teachings. After finishing a rough draft in his early fifties, he continued to refine it the rest of his life, editing and amending it.

TWOFOLD REVELATION *(NISHU JINSHIN)*

The state of mind of one who has been saved by Amida. When we are saved by the wondrous power of Amida's Vow, and our darkness of mind is eliminated, two things become clear: "Beyond any shadow of doubt, it has been revealed to me that I will go to Hell for all eternity" (Revelation of the true self) and "Beyond any shadow of doubt, it has been revealed to me that I will go to Paradise for all eternity" (Revelation of the truth of the Vow of Amida). Both of these become clear simultaneously and remain so until death. They are known as the "unified twofold revelation of the self and the Vow of Amida" or simply "twofold revelation."

BIBLIOGRAPHY

WESTERN LANGUAGES

Alighieri, Dante. "The Divine Comedy." Translated by Charles S. Singleton. In *Great Books of the Western World*, Vol. 19, Dante/Chaucer. Chicago: Encyclopaedia Britannica, Inc., 1990.

"Attacks on Homeless Reported Nationwide." The Associated Press, January 19, 2006. Available at the website of *USA Today*.

Bierce, Ambrose. *The Devil's Dictionary*. Ware, England: Wordsworth Editions Ltd, 1996.

Brent, David. "Suicide in Youth." The Nation's Voice on Mental Illness. June 2003. Available at the website of NAMI (the National Alliance on Mental Illness).

Busse, Karl. "Over the Mountains." Unpublished translation by William Reis of *"Über den Bergen."*

Camus, Albert. *The Myth of Sisyphus*. Translated by Justin O'Brien. London: Penguin Books Ltd, 2000.

Cassirer, Ernst. *An Essay on Man: An Introduction to a Philosophy of Human Culture*. New Haven and London: Yale University Press, 1992.

"CDC Reports Latest Data on Suicide Behaviors, Risk Factors, and Prevention." Centers for Disease Control and Prevention. Press Release, June 10, 2004. Available at the website of CDC.

Chekhov, Anton. "Ward No. 6." In *Ward No. 6 and Other Stories*. Translated by Constance Garnett. New York: Barnes & Noble, Inc., 2003.

Csikszentmihalyi, Mihaly. *Flow: The Psychology of Optimal Experience*. New York: Harper & Row, Publishers, Inc., 1990.

Didion, Joan. *The Year of Magical Thinking*. New York: Alfred A. Knopf, 2005.

Distel, Anne. *Renoir: A Sensuous Vision*. Translated by Lory Frankel. New York: Harry N. Abrams, Inc., 1995.

Dostoevsky, Fyodor. *Memoirs from the House of the Dead*. Translated by Jessie Coulson. New York: Oxford University Press Inc., 2001.

Durkheim, Emile. *Suicide: A Study in Sociology*. Translated by John A. Spaulding & George Simpson. New York: The Free Press, 1979.

Einstein, Albert. *The World As I See It*. Translated by Alan Harris. New York: The Philosophical Library, Inc., 1949.

Emerson, Ralph Waldo. "Fate." In *Selected Writings of Ralph Waldo Emerson*. New York: Penguin Group (USA) Inc., 2003.

Foot, Philippa. "Moral Relativism." In *Moral Dilemmas and Other Topics in Moral Philosophy*. New York: Oxford University Press Inc., 2002.

Frankl, Viktor Emil. *Man's Search for Meaning: An Introduction to Logotherapy*. Translated by Ilse Lasch. New York: Simon & Schuster, Inc., 1984.

Fraser, Jill Andresky. *White-Collar Sweatshop: The Deterioration of Work and Its Rewards in Corporate America*. New York: W. W. Norton & Company, Inc., 2002.

Goethe, Johann Wolfgang von. *Faust,* Part One. Translated by David Luke. Oxford: Oxford University Press, 1998.

———. *The Sorrows of Young Werther*. Translated by Thomas Carlyle and R. D. Boylan. Mineola, N.Y.: Dover Publications, Inc., 2002.

"In Harm's Way: Suicide in America." National Institute of Mental Health. NIH Publication No. 03–4594. Printed January 2001; revised May 2003.

James, William. *The Varieties of Religious Experience: A Study in Human Nature; Being the Gifford Lectures on Natural Religion Delivered at Edinburgh in 1901–1902*. Mineola, N.Y.: Dover Publications, Inc., 2002.

Jung, Carl. *The Undiscovered Self.* Translated by R. F. C. Hull. New York: Penguin Group (USA) Inc., 2006.

Kierkegaard, Søren. *The Sickness Unto Death: A Christian Psychological Exposition for Edification and Awakening by Anti-Climacus*. Translated by Alastair Hannay. London: Penguin Books Ltd, 2004.

Kitagawa, Hiroshi, and Bruce T. Tsuchida, trans. *The Tale of the Heike*, Vol. 1. Tokyo: University of Tokyo Press, 1975.

Kohn, Alfie. *No Contest: The Case Against Competition*. New York: Houghton Mifflin Company, 1992.

Leavy, Walter. "The Price of Fame: Stardom's Other Side." *Ebony*, September 1994, 54–59.

Miller, Arthur. *Death of a Salesman*. London: Penguin Books Ltd, 2000.

Moskowitz, Eva S. *In Therapy We Trust: America's Obsession with Self-Fulfillment*. Baltimore: The Johns Hopkins University Press, 2001.

Nietzsche, Friedrich. *On the Genealogy of Morals: A Polemic: By Way of Clarification and Supplement to My Last Book Beyond Good and Evil*. Translated by Douglas Smith. Oxford: Oxford University Press, 1998.

———. *Thus Spake Zarathustra: A Book for All and None*. Translated by Thomas

Common. In *The Complete Works of Friedrich Nietzsche*, Vol. 11. New York: Russell and Russell, Inc., 1964.

Pascal, Blaise. *Pensées*. Translated by W. F. Trotter. Mineola, N.Y.: Dover Publications, Inc., 2003.

Plato. "Gorgias" and "Symposium." Translated by Benjamin Jowett. In *Great Books of the Western World*, Vol. 7, Plato. Chicago: Encyclopaedia Britannica, Inc., 1952.

Rilke, Rainer Maria. "The Neighbor." In *Selected Poems*. Translated by C. F. MacIntyre. Berkeley and Los Angeles: University of California Press, 2001.

Rousseau, Jean-Jacques. "The Social Contract." In *Discourse on Political Economy and The Social Contract*. Translated by Christopher Betts. New York: Oxford University Press Inc., 1999.

Ruben, Harvey L. *Competing: Understanding and Winning the Strategic Games We All Play*. New York: Lippincott & Crowell, Publishers, 1980.

Russell, Bertrand. *The Conquest of Happiness*. New York: W. W. Norton & Company, Inc., 1996.

Sartre, Jean-Paul. *Being and Nothingness: A Phenomenological Essay on Ontology*. Translated by Hazel E. Barnes. New York: Simon & Schuster, Inc., 1992.

Schopenhauer, Arthur. *The World as Will and Representation*, Vol. 1. Translated by E. F. J. Payne. Mineola, N.Y.: Dover Publications, Inc., 1969.

Shakespeare, William. *Hamlet*. London: Penguin Books Ltd, 1996.

———. *King Lear*. Surrey: Thomas Nelson and Sons Ltd, 1997.

———. *Measure for Measure*. Cambridge: Cambridge University Press, 1993.

———. *Romeo and Juliet*. London: Penguin Books Ltd, 1996.

Singer, Irving. *Meaning in Life: The Creation of Value*. New York: The Free Press, 1992.

Tillich, Paul. *The Courage to Be*. New Haven and London: Yale University Press, 2000.

Tolstoy, Leo. "A Confession." In *A Confession and Other Religious Writings*. Translated by Jane Kentish. London: Penguin Books Ltd, 1987.

Trump, Donald J. and Charles Leerhsen. *Surviving at the Top*. New York: Random House, Inc., 1990.

Watson, James D. *The Double Helix: A Personal Account of the Discovery of the Structure of DNA*. New York: Simon & Schuster, Inc., 2001.

Zeldin, Theodore. *An Intimate History of Humanity*. New York: HarperCollins Publishers, Inc., 1996.

JAPANESE—GENERAL

Akutagawa, Ryunosuke. "*Kumo no ito*" [The Spider's Thread]. In *Kumo no ito, Toshishun* [The Spider's Thread, Toshishun]. Tokyo: Shinchosha, 1968.

———. "*Shuju no kotoba*" [Words of a Dwarf]. In *Shuju no kotoba, Saiho no hito* [Words of a Dwarf, Man of the West]. Tokyo: Shinchosha, 1968.

Eto, Jun. "*Tsuma to watashi*" [My Wife and I]. *Bungei shunju*, May 1999, 94–133.

Hilty, Karl. *Kofukuron* [On Happiness], Vol. 3. Translated by Heisaku Kusama and Kunitaro Yamato. Tokyo: Iwanami Shoten, 1965.

Iijima, Hanjuro. *Katsushika Hokusai den* [Katsushika Hokusai: A Biography]. Tokyo: Hosukaku, 1893.

Itsuki, Hiroyuki. *Jinsei no mokuteki* [Life's Purpose]. Tokyo: Gentosha, 1999.

Kamei, Katsuichiro. "*Shinran*." In *Kamei Katsuichiro senshu*, Vol. 1: *Watakushi no shukyokan* [Collected Works of Kamei Katsuichiro, Vol. 1: My Views on Religion]. Tokyo: Kodansha, 1965.

"*Kin medarutte shiawase nanka ja nakatta*" [The Gold Medal Wasn't Happiness]. *Josei sebun*. June 10, 1999, 43–46.

Kishimoto, Hideo. *Shi o mitsumeru kokoro—Gan to tatakatta junenkan* [The Mind Trained on Death: Ten Years Fighting Cancer]. Tokyo: Kodansha, 1973.

Miyadai, Shinji. *Jiyu na shinseiki, fujiyu na anata* [The Free New Century, the Unfree You]. Tokyo: Mediafactory Inc., 2000.

Miyadai, Shinji and Seiji Fujii. *Utsukushiki shonen no riyu naki jisatsu* [The Groundless Suicide of a Beautiful Youth]. Tokyo: Mediafactory Inc., 1999.

Miyadai, Shinji, Yoshiki Fujii, and Akio Nakamori. *Shinseiki no riaru* [Reality of the New Century]. Tokyo: Asukashinsha, 1997.

Morotomi, Yoshihiko. *Munashisa no shinrigaku—Naze mitasarenai no ka* [The Psychology of Emptiness: Why Are We Unfulfilled?]. Tokyo: Kodansha, 1997.

Murakami, Haruki. *Kaiten mokuba no deddo hiito* [Dead Heat on a Carousel], Tokyo: Kodansha, 1988.

Natsume, Soseki. *Kusamakura* [Pillow of Grass]. Tokyo: Shinchosha, 1950.

Ninomiya, Seijun. "*Onizuka Katsuya: Dokuhaku yojikan*" [Katsuya Onizuka: Four Hours of Confessions]. *Shukan bunshun*. November 17, 1994, 181–85.

Ohira, Ken. *Yasashisa no seishin byori* [Psychopathy of Tenderness]. Tokyo: Iwanami Shoten, 1995.

Okushiro, Yoshiharu. *Kyogo seerusu no himitsu* [The Secret of Champion Sales], Tokyo: Jitsugyo no Nihonsha, 1973.

Seneca. "*Kofuku na jinsei ni tsuite*" [On the Happy Life]. Translated by Motozo

Motegi. In *Jinsei no mijikasa ni tsuite* [On the Shortness of Life]. Tokyo: Iwanami Shoten, 1980.

Tanaka, Tsuruaki. *"Jinsei no mokuteki wa nan desu ka"* [What Is the Purpose of Life?]. Financial Report for the Construction Research Institute, March 1999.

WRITINGS OF SHINRAN

Goshosoku shu [Collected Letters]. In *Shinshu shiryo shusei* [The Collected Texts of Shin Buddhism], Vol. 1. Edited by Mitsuyuki Ishida and Joryu Chiba. Kyoto: Dohosha, 1974.

Gutoku sho [Gutoku's Notes]. In *Shinshu shiryo shusei*, Vol. 1.

Hitanjukkai wasan [Hymns of Lament and Reflection]. In *Shinshu shogyo zensho* [The Sacred Literatures of Shin Buddhism], Vol. 2. Edited by Shinshu Shogyo Zensho Hensanjo. Kyoto: Oyagi Kobundo, 1941.

Ichinen tanen mon'i [Concerning Single Invocation and Many Invocations]. In *Shinshu shiryo shusei*, Vol. 1.

Jodo wasan [Hymns on the Pure Land]. In *Shinshu shogyo zensho*, Vol. 2.

Koso wasan [Hymns on the Masters]. In *Shinshu shogyo zensho*, Vol. 2.

Kyogyoshinsho [Teaching, Practice, Faith, Enlightenment]. In *Shinshu shogyo zensho*, Vol. 2.

Mattosho [Lamp for the Latter Age]. In *Shinshu shiryo shusei*, Vol. 1.

Shozomatsu wasan [Hymns on the Three Ages]. In *Shinshu shogyo zensho*, Vol. 2.

Songo shinzo meimon [In Praise of the Sacred Name and the True Image]. In *Shinshu shiryo shusei*, Vol. 1.

Yuishin sho mon'i [Notes on "Essentials of Faith Alone"]. In *Shinshu shogyo zensho*, Vol. 2.

OTHER CLASSICAL TEXTS

Daichido ron [*Ta-chih-tu-lun* or Great Perfection of Wisdom Treatise] (Skt., *Mahāprajñāpāramitopadeśa*). Attributed to Nāgārjuna and translated from Sanskrit to Chinese by Kumārajīva.

Daimuryoju kyo [The Larger Sutra of Infinite Life] (Skt., *Sukhāvatī-vyūha*).

Gaijasho [Notes Rectifying Heresy] by Kakunyo. In *Shinshu shiryo shusei*, Vol. 1.

Godensho [The Biography] by Kakunyo. In *Shinshu shogyo zensho*, Vol. 3. Edited by Shinshu Shogyo Zensho Hensanjo. Kyoto: Oyagi Kobundo, 1941.

Gobunsho [The Letters] by Rennyo. In *Shinshu shiryo shusei*, Vol. 2. Edited by Osamu Katata. Kyoto: Dohosha, 1977.

Kanmuryoju kyo [The Sutra of Contemplation on the Buddha of Infinite Life] (Skt., *Amitāyur-dhyāna-sūtra*).

Kudensho [Notes on Oral Transmissions] by Kakunyo. In *Shinshu shiryo shusei*, Vol. 1.

Shujisho [Notes on Steadfast Holding] by Kakunyo. In *Shinshu shiryo shusei*, Vol. 1.

Tandoku mon [Panegyric] by Zonkaku. In *Shinshu shiryo shusei*, Vol. 1.

Tannisho [Lamenting the Deviations], attributed to Yuienbo. In *Shinshu shiryo shusei*, Vol. 1.

INDEX

NOTE: Bold numbers indicate entries in the Glossary.